Lift

EXPERIENCING THE ELEVATED LIFE

TONY COOKE

Harrison House

Tulsa, OK

20 19 18 17 10 9 8 7 6 5 4 3 2 1

Lift
ISBN: 978-168031-130-3

Broken Arrow, OK 74014

Published by:
Harrison House Publishers
Tulsa, OK 74145
www.harrisonhouse.com

Love lifted me!

Love lifted me!

When nothing else could help,

Love lifted me.[1]

[1] James Rowe, *Love Lifted Me* (Public Domain, 1912).

Contents

Introduction

At the time of this writing, troubling news reports continue to surface about dangerously high levels of radiation seeping from the Fukushima nuclear reactor in Japan. Serious damage occurred at that nuclear facility in 2011 when a large earthquake triggered a tsunami, which in turn hit the plant. Years after the initial tragedy, the reactor is still releasing radiation. Scientists say that low levels of seaborne radiation have even reached the west coast of the United States.

No sane person would consider the Fukushima tragedy to be a positive event, nor would anyone consider the ongoing leakage of radiation to be good news. However, the idea of a powerful event followed by a continuing release of power is nothing new. The power of God raised Jesus from the dead, and that same power continues to flow from Jesus' resurrection to those who believe in him. This resurrection life not only makes us new people, but it also provides significant *lift* for our lives, enabling us to live an elevated or higher quality of life.

The historical resurrection of Jesus is indispensable to the Christian faith, and so is the future resurrection of our bodies. Between these two landmark events, we live our life in the here and now. This book explains how the power flowing from Jesus' resurrection in the past and the hope we hold as we move toward the resurrection of our bodies in the future should dramatically affect our daily lives in the present.

Despite God's good plan, many believers are not nearly as affected by *lift*—the resurrection power available to them—as they could be. For example, someone recently said to me, "I just talked with a person who has been out of church for a long time, so I asked him why. He explained an offense that had been taken, something minor, and that he hadn't been back to church since. Why would someone allow such an insignificant thing to sidetrack him and keep him from God's best?"

When this question was posed to me, I thought of the many stories I have heard over the years about people who allow themselves to be distracted, snagged, sidetracked, and bogged down. Some eventually got unstuck and resumed making spiritual progress, reestablishing their forward momentum. Unfortunately, many others continued to flounder and stagnate, never regaining their footing or positive traction in their spiritual journey. When this happens, people live far below their God-given potential and destiny.

After reflecting for a moment, I said, "When people hold on to something like that, it is often evidence of the sad fact that they see nothing better—there is nothing more to which they aspire—so they cling to the rags of the past. Their current condition is all they see for themselves." I also shared that in order to move beyond past pain, it is tremendously helpful if we have future purpose. When people perceive a compelling destiny for their future or are captivated by a sense of meaning in their present, it is easier for them to let go of and move beyond their past. In this way, resurrection lifts us out of death into new life.

The resurrection theme appears throughout Scripture. Even when the word "resurrection" does not appear, God's love and influence are consistently lifting people, bringing them out of death into new life. Consider Peter. When the pressure was on, he denied that he even knew Jesus. Peter was crushed and devastated by his failure to remain true to the Lord; his hope died. However, Jesus (newly raised himself) brought resurrection life to Peter's crushed spirit. Jesus conveyed and extended life, hope, and a new beginning to Peter (John 21:15-17). How many times has this same type of lift occurred throughout Scripture? How many times has it happened in your life?

Think about it. God does not want us stuck as prisoners, enslaved to our past. Nor does he want us frozen in the present, unable to establish positive traction and momentum in our lives. But God wants to do more than just lift us out of problems; he wants to empower us with purpose.

We were created for something greater, higher, and better than we have ever experienced. Yet most people live far below their God-given potential and purpose. There is an "upward call" that God has for us—an elevating lift of resurrection life—and as we learn to heed and cultivate that upward call, we will experience an upgraded and enhanced life. God did not create us to wallow and grovel; he designed us to ascend and soar.

This book is written to form and reinforce the belief in our hearts that God greatly desires to lift us, and to expound on how we can each live an elevated life. One of the most important truths of Scripture is that God will meet us wherever we are. If we are down, he will meet us there. But that is not where he wants us to stay.

The first section deals with facts presented in the Bible as they pertain to doctrine about the resurrection of Jesus, the future resurrection of believers, and the resurrection life we can experience in the here and now. Doctrine is not a mere collection of information; it is meant to affect our everyday life.

Section II explains how the lifting nature of God affected great characters in the Bible. Paul, Joseph, Nehemiah, and Gideon all experienced elevation because of the operation of God's Spirit in their lives. Each of these individuals fulfilled a divine purpose he never could have accomplished without the lift and elevation that came from God's Spirit. Again, the word "resurrection" may not appear in many of these stories, but the *concept* of resurrection—of God's raising people higher—is constantly at work.

Section III provides instruction and inspiration for living an elevated life. God's ways are higher than ours, and these chapters exhort and encourage us to move into those higher ways.

You will find some additional material at the end of every chapter. First, there is a "Resurrection Declaration." This allows you to personalize and verbalize key truths from each chapter in a devotional manner. Second, "Bonus Quotes" add rich insights from others to the content of the chapter. Third, "Lyrics that Lift" cite selected verses from various hymns, highlighting resurrection themes that have encouraged the saints throughout the centuries. Finally, each chapter concludes with "Questions for Reflection and Discussion."

Before delving into the following chapters, consider these verses that reveal what God wants to do in the lives of his people:

DEUTERONOMY 28:1
1 Now it shall come to pass, if you diligently obey the voice of the Lord your God, to observe carefully all his commandments which I command you today, that the Lord your God will set you high above all nations of the earth.

JOB 5:11
11 He sets on high those who are lowly, and those who mourn are lifted to safety.

PSALM 3:3
3 But you, O Lord, are a shield for me, my glory and the one who lifts up my head.

PSALM 18:33
33 He makes my feet like the feet of deer, and sets me on my high places.

PSALM 91:4
4 Because he has set his love upon me, therefore I will deliver him; I will set him on high, because he has known my name.

ISAIAH 40:31 (*NLT*)
31 But those who trust in the Lord will find new strength. They will soar high on wings like eagles. They will run and not grow weary. They will walk and not faint.

MATTHEW 23:12
12 And whoever exalts himself will be humbled, and he who humbles himself will be exalted.

JAMES 4:10
10 Humble yourselves in the sight of the Lord, and He will lift you up.

The Bible makes it abundantly clear that God wants to lift and exalt his people, to set us on high, and to cause us to walk in high places! May the insights presented on the following pages empower you to truly experience an elevated life.

SECTION I

Resurrection: The Doctrine of *Lift*

CHAPTER ONE

Resurrection Past and Resurrection Future

"This is the message of the resurrection.
Life springs forth from death.
A desert becomes a garden.
Beauty transcends the ugly.
Love overcomes hatred.
A tomb is emptied. The grim and
haunting outline of a cross is swallowed
in the glow of an Easter morning sunrise."[2]

— Max Anders

Those who think that all religions are the same miss a glaring difference between Christianity and other belief systems. What gloriously distinguishes the gospel of Jesus Christ from other faiths is the literal, physical resurrection of Christ himself. Not only is Christ's resurrection

[2] Max Anders, *What You Need to Know About Jesus in 12 Lessons* (Nashville, Thomas Nelson Publishers, 1995), 155.

inextricably woven into the very fabric of Scripture, but it is also the very basis for the uniqueness of our faith. Tony Evans brilliantly explains:

> The Resurrection places Jesus Christ in a class by Himself. It makes Him unique. Other religions can compete with Christianity on some things. They can say, for example, "Your founder gave you a holy book? Our founder gave us a holy book. Your founder has a large following? So does ours. You have buildings where people come to worship your God? We have buildings where people come to worship our god." But Christians can say, "All of that may be true, but our Founder rose from the dead!"[3]

The fact of Jesus' resurrection is monumental, and its implications are all-important to our temporal and eternal well-being. The Apostle Paul teaches that Jesus "was handed over to die because of our sins, and he was raised to life to make us right with God" (Rom. 4:25, *NLT*). We have right standing with God because he raised Jesus from the dead! We need to recognize and believe in the historical reality of Jesus' death and resurrection, but we must not miss the vital fact in this: It was *for us* that Jesus died and was raised. His blood secured our forgiveness; his resurrection provides our justification. In other words, as we trust in what Jesus did for us, we are placed in right standing with God.

At the church I grew up in, we recited the Apostles' Creed every Sunday. While Jesus' original band of apostles did not actually write this ancient text, its concise and powerful language expresses the chief elements of their teaching as it was handed down to successive generations of believers. Though I did not fully appreciate the gravity or the significance of these statements early in my life, I am glad that I repeated them over

[3] Tony Evans, *Who Is This King of Glory: Experiencing the Fullness of Christ's Work In Our Lives* (Chicago, Moody Press, 1999), 81-82.

and over again as a young person. When I came to a personal, quickened faith in Jesus, these concepts were familiar to me and served as tremendous reference points as I studied Scripture and grew in the Lord:

> I believe in God, the Father Almighty, the Creator of heaven and earth, and in Jesus Christ, His only Son, our Lord: Who was conceived of the Holy Spirit, born of the Virgin Mary, suffered under Pontius Pilate, was crucified, died, and was buried. He descended into hell. The third day *He arose again from the dead.* He ascended into heaven and sits at the right hand of God the Father Almighty, whence He shall come to judge the living and the dead. I believe in the Holy Spirit, the holy catholic church[4], the communion of saints, the forgiveness of sins, *the resurrection of the body*, and life everlasting (emphasis mine).

I emphasized the two references to resurrection. The first is a reference to Jesus' resurrection—the historical fact. The second usage pertains to our coming resurrection—a future hope. These momentous occasions rightfully represent two of the most significant teachings in the New Testament. Let us examine each of these individually.

Resurrection Past—The Raising of Christ

During his earthly ministry, Jesus staked the validity of his ministry and his entire future on this simple promise: "I will rise again!" Paul considers the fact that Jesus "rose again the third day according to the Scripture" (1 Cor. 15:4) to be of absolute and primary importance in the gospel. He even tells the Corinthian Church, "If Christ is not risen, your faith is futile; you are still in your sins" (1 Cor. 15:17). In other words, if there is

[4] The word "catholic" here does not refer to the Roman Catholic Church, but rather, to the Universal Church—the entire Body of Christ as a whole.

no resurrection, there is no gospel. Let me state this plainly: Any form or version of Christianity that does not have Jesus' death, burial, and resurrection at its center and core represents a radical departure from the doctrine presented in the Bible.

When believers reflect on the Day of Pentecost detailed in Acts chapter 2, they naturally think of the great outpouring of the Holy Spirit, which is understandable. What they tend to overlook, though, is the phenomenal message that Peter preached—a sermon that saw 3,000 people surrender their lives to the Lordship of Jesus Christ. Peter spoke convincingly of the death, burial, and resurrection of Jesus. In his sermon, Peter proclaims, "God released him from the horrors of death and raised him back to life, for death could not keep him in its grip" (Acts 2:24, *NLT*). Peter proceeds to quote an Old Testament prophecy in which King David states, "You will not leave my soul among the dead or allow your Holy One to rot in the grave" (Acts 2:27, *NLT*). Inspired by the Holy Spirit, Peter makes a shocking interpretation of that passage:

ACTS 2:29-33 (*NLT*)

29 You can be sure that the patriarch David wasn't referring to himself, for he died and was buried, and his tomb is still here among us.

30 But he was a prophet, and he knew God had promised with an oath that one of David's own descendants would sit on his throne.

31 David was looking into the future and speaking of the Messiah's resurrection. He was saying that God would not leave him among the dead or allow his body to rot in the grave.

32 God raised Jesus from the dead, and we are all witnesses of this.

33 Now he is exalted to the place of highest honor in heaven, at God's right hand.

Resurrection is more than just the reviving of the physical body. Remember, Jesus raised three people from the dead during his earthly ministry—and all of those people eventually died again. When Jesus was resurrected, it was something more than what others had experienced—he was raised to new life, *never to die again*! The risen Jesus triumphantly declares, "I am he who lives, and was dead, and behold, I am alive forevermore" (Rev. 1:18).

Jesus was not raised as a ghost or some kind of vapor; he inhabited the same physical body in which he had lived during his time upon the earth, but his physical body was also a glorified and transformed body. Luke explains this concept in his written account of Jesus' appearance to his disciples after his resurrection:

LUKE 24:36-43

36 Jesus himself stood in the midst of them, and said to them, "Peace to you."

37 But they were terrified and frightened, and supposed they had seen a spirit.

38 And he said to them, "Why are you troubled? And why do doubts arise in your hearts?

39 Behold my hands and my feet, that it is I myself. Handle me and see, for a spirit does not have flesh and bones as you see I have."

40 When he had said this, he showed them his hands and his feet.

41 But while they still did not believe for joy, and marveled, he said to them, "Have you any food here?"

42 So they gave him a piece of a broiled fish and some honeycomb.

43 And he took it and ate in their presence.

John's Gospel records an additional aspect of this same account—Jesus' breathing on the disciples and imparting the Holy Spirit to them:

JOHN 20:19-20, 22

19 Jesus came and stood in the midst, and said to them, "Peace be with you."

20 When he had said this, he showed them his hands and his side.

22 He breathed on them, and said to them, "Receive the Holy Spirit."

Jesus further reinforces the physicality and reality of his resurrection when he speaks to Thomas (who is encountering the resurrected Jesus for the first time). Jesus tells Thomas, "Reach your finger here, and look at my hands; and reach your hand here, and put it into my side. Do not be unbelieving, but believing" (John 20:27). Scripture clearly indicates that Jesus engaged in many normal human physical activities such as breathing, walking, standing, talking, and eating. The resurrection aimed to quicken his physical body, not do away with it.

The resurrection of Jesus' body was the fulfillment of what he himself had predicted.[5] Neither his death nor his resurrection was accidental—they were part of God's eternal, redemptive plan for humanity. Romans 1:4 states that Jesus was "declared to be the Son of God with power according to the Spirit of holiness, by the resurrection from the dead." His resurrection is the basis for all of our hope! Jesus proclaims, "Because I live, you will live also" (John 14:19).

---

[5] Jesus predicted his resurrection in many passages such as Matthew 12:40; 16:21; 27:62-64 and John 2:18-22; 10:17-18.

Resurrection Future—
The Glorious Transformation of Our Bodies

The Apostles' Creed articulates belief in both the resurrection of Jesus and the resurrection of our bodies. This is absolutely what the Bible teaches, and there is a direct, indissoluble connection between the two resurrections: Jesus' resurrection in the past is the premise, prototype, and basis for our resurrection in the future. Paul explains the connection this way:

1 CORINTHIANS 15:20-23

20 But now Christ is risen from the dead, and has become the firstfruits of those who have fallen asleep.

21 For since by man came death, by Man also came the resurrection of the dead.

22 For as in Adam all die, even so in Christ all shall be made alive.

23 But each one in his own order: Christ the firstfruits, afterward those who are Christ's at his coming.

Paul's audience understood the idea of firstfruits: They were the first portion of the harvest and represented the remainder of the harvest that would follow. Referring to Christ as firstfruits indicates that Jesus' resurrection testified of and promised a great future resurrection.

The idea of a future resurrection is not something that Paul invented; rather, the Old Testament strongly attests to it—as does Jesus himself in the gospel accounts. Consider these powerful statements:

- Job proclaims, "For I know that my Redeemer lives, and he shall stand at last on the earth; And after my skin is destroyed, this I know, that in my flesh I shall see God" (Job 19:25-26).
- Isaiah declares, "But those who die in the Lord will live; their bodies will rise again! Those who sleep in the earth will rise up and sing for joy!" (Isa. 26:19, *NLT*).

- Daniel writes, "And many of those who sleep in the dust of the earth shall awake, some to everlasting life, some to shame and everlasting contempt" (Dan. 12:2).
- Jesus prophesies, "The hour is coming in which all who are in the graves will hear his voice and come forth—those who have done good, to the resurrection of life, and those who have done evil, to the resurrection of condemnation" (John 5:28-29). Shortly after, Jesus states, "And this is the will of him who sent me, that everyone who sees the Son and believes in Him may have everlasting life; and I will raise him up at the last day" (John 6:40).

The Apostle Paul provides the greatest detail of any New Testament writer concerning the future resurrection of believers. His Spirit-inspired words of truth have brought tremendous comfort to countless individuals at the gravesides of loved ones:

1 CORINTHIANS 15:51-54
51 Behold, I tell you a mystery: We shall not all sleep, but we shall all be changed—

52 in a moment, in the twinkling of an eye, at the last trumpet. For the trumpet will sound, and the dead will be raised incorruptible, and we shall be changed.

53 For this corruptible must put on incorruption, and this mortal must put on immortality.

54 So when this corruptible has put on incorruption, and this mortal has put on immortality, then shall be brought to pass the saying that is written: "Death is swallowed up in victory."

1 THESSALONIANS 4:14-17 (*NLT*)
14 For since we believe that Jesus died and was raised to life again, we also believe that when Jesus returns, God will bring back with him the believers who have died.

15 We tell you this directly from the Lord: We who are still living when the Lord returns will not meet him ahead of those who have died.

16 The Lord himself will come down from heaven with a commanding shout, with the voice of the archangel, and with the trumpet call of God. First, the Christians who have died will rise from their graves.

17 Then, together with them, we who are still alive and remain on the earth will be caught up in the clouds to meet the Lord in the air.

This promise to be resurrected and reunited with the Lord provides hope to the believer and buoys our faith during hard times.

During the Apostle Paul's ministry, many people—especially the Greeks—believed that the body was evil; it was a common cultural perception to view the body as a type of prison from which death would bring welcome deliverance. Therefore, it was a radical idea that God's eternal plan would include our body along with our spirit and soul, but this truth is exactly what the New Testament reveals. Paul again makes this clear when he writes to the Church at Corinth:

2 CORINTHIANS 5:4 (*NLT*)

4 While we live in these earthly bodies, we groan and sigh, but it's not that we want to die and get rid of these bodies that clothe us. Rather, we want to put on our new bodies so that these dying bodies will be swallowed up by life.

The New Testament not only teaches the immortality of the inner man (the spirit and soul), but also the resurrection of the physical body.

PHILIPPIANS 3:20-21 (*NLT*)

20 We are citizens of heaven, where the Lord Jesus Christ lives. And we are eagerly waiting for him to return as our Savior.

21 He will take our weak mortal bodies and change them into glorious bodies like his own, using the same power with which he will bring everything under his control.

The past resurrection of Jesus and the future resurrection of believers stand as anchors of the Christian's faith and hope. In the next two chapters, we will look at what the believer can experience *now*, in between these two great pillars—the past resurrection of Jesus and the future resurrection of our bodies.

A Resurrection Declaration

The Apostles' Creed: "I believe in God, the Father Almighty, the Creator of heaven and earth, and in Jesus Christ, His only Son, our Lord: Who was conceived of the Holy Spirit, born of the Virgin Mary, suffered under Pontius Pilate, was crucified, died, and was buried. He descended into hell. The third day He arose again from the dead. He ascended into heaven and sits at the right hand of God the Father Almighty, whence He shall come to judge the living and the dead. I believe in the Holy Spirit, the holy catholic church, the communion of saints, the forgiveness of sins, the resurrection of the body, and life everlasting."

Bonus Quotes

"The resurrection of Jesus Christ was necessary to establish the truth of his mission and put the stamp of all-conquering power on his gospel."

—E. M. Bounds

"Our Lord has written the promise of resurrection, not in books alone, but in every leaf in springtime."

—Martin Luther

"Let every man and woman count himself immortal. Let him catch the revelation of Jesus in his resurrection. Let him say not merely, 'Christ is risen,' but 'I shall rise.'"

—Phillips Brooks

"The resurrection is not merely important to the historic Christian faith; without it, there would be no Christianity.
It is the singular doctrine that elevates Christianity above all other world religions."

—Adrian Rogers

 Lyrics that Lift: Hymns of the Resurrection

From "Christ the Lord is Risen Today" by Charles Wesley (1739)

Christ the Lord is risen today, Alleluia!

Earth and heaven in chorus say, Alleluia!

Raise your joys and triumphs high, Alleluia!

Sing, ye heavens, and earth reply, Alleluia!

Soar we now where Christ has led, Alleluia!

Following our exalted Head, Alleluia!

Made like him, like him we rise, Alleluia!

Ours the cross, the grave, the skies, Alleluia!

 Questions for Reflection and Discussion

1. How does the resurrection of Christ set Christianity apart from all other belief systems? Why does the resurrection matter?
2. Jesus was raised from the dead, but he also raised others from the dead—such as Lazarus. What is the difference between Jesus' resurrection and that of others in Scripture?
3. What might you say to someone who believes that Jesus was *spiritually* raised from the dead but not *physically* raised?
4. When Jesus is referred to as "the firstfruits" (1 Cor. 15:20-23), what are the implications for us? What does his resurrection have to do with us and our future destiny?
5. Consider the difference between the way the ancient Greeks viewed the human body and the view presented in the New Testament. What responsibilities does the New Testament perspective create for believers regarding the way we ought to treat our body?

CHAPTER TWO

Resurrection Power in the Here and Now

Resurrection is a historical fact to be celebrated,
a future event to be anticipated,
and a current reality to be experienced.

If there is one word in Scripture that decisively communicates God's overwhelming determination to lift his people, it is the word *resurrection*. Even though the most important day on the Church calendar is Easter—the Sunday when Christians celebrate Jesus' resurrection from the dead, it can be argued that the *demonstration* of Jesus' resurrection power in the lives of his followers is far from what it should be. People who merely give a respectful nod to Christ's resurrection once a year do not experience his resurrection power on a daily basis. The average Christian knows of Jesus' resurrection as historical fact and is aware of the resurrection of the dead—that future event when believers will receive glorified bodies.[6] However, believers also need to experience and apply this resurrection power to their daily lives in the here and now.

When Jesus encountered Martha four days after the death of her brother Lazarus, a very revealing conversation took place regarding the topic of resurrection:

JOHN 11:23-25 (*NLT*)

23 Jesus told her, "Your brother will rise again."

24 "Yes," Martha said, "he will rise when everyone else rises, at the last day."

25 Jesus told her, "I am the resurrection and the life. Anyone who believes in me will live, even after dying."

Jesus then proceeds to raise Lazarus from the dead. Though it was not the ultimate resurrection that will occur when the Lord returns in the future (Lazarus would eventually die again), it was nonetheless a display of resurrection power that was shown *before* the eschatological resurrection that we discussed in the previous chapter. Martha's initial response to Jesus (that Lazarus would be raised on the last day) is understandable, but Jesus reveals to her a deeper reality: Resurrection is not merely a future eschatological event; it is embodied and personified in Jesus himself!

Regarding this exchange between Jesus and Martha, preacher and author Vance Havner writes, "Martha believed in the resurrection, but Jesus moved her from the doctrinal to the personal: 'I am the resurrection.'

[6] The Bible teaches that the unjust will also be resurrected (e.g., Dan 12:2; John 5:28-29; Acts 24:15; Rev 20:4-5, 11-15), but that is not the focus of this book.

The resurrection is not an 'It'—'I am the resurrection.' We stop too often with 'It.'"[7]

I am not disputing the reality of the future resurrection that will occur when Jesus returns. I am simply asserting that there can also be displays of resurrection life and resurrection power that profoundly affect and influence our lives in the here and now.

It seems that people tend to assume that God's greatest and richest blessings are either in the distant past or in the distant future. This assumption is understandable; after all, who could deny the phenomenal blessing of Jesus' ministry here on earth or the glories of the eternal realm? We need to avoid, though, the misdirected focus exhibited by Martha—thinking that resurrection power is exclusively relegated to a far-off future event, and failing to realize that at least an aspect of resurrection power is currently available that can affect our lives right now.

What About the Here and Now?

Believers who speak only about the glorious things that happened when Jesus was alive and the wonderful things that will happen when we get to heaven can potentially miss out on many present-tense blessings of resurrection life and power. Jesus, who *is* the Resurrection and the Life, is also "the same yesterday, today, and forever" (Heb. 13:8). Someone once said, "I want a little bit of heaven to go to heaven in." This phrase is another way that believers express their desire to experience some resurrection power now while they await *the* resurrection.

---

[7] Vance Havner, *The Vance Havner Quote Book: Sparkling Gems From the Most Quoted Preacher in America*, Compiled by Dennis J. Hester (Grand Rapids: Baker Book House, 1986), 190.

But is such a desire justified, and is there a biblical basis for expecting and experiencing such power in our lives today? Does the Bible teach that we can experience resurrection-based life—resurrection-based *lift*—on a daily basis?

Would it even matter if resurrection power (lift) were available to us in the here and now? I believe it matters greatly. Thank God for the historical resurrection of Jesus, and thank God for the future promised resurrection of our bodies. But we all have to deal with the challenges in the present.

Imagine living halfway between two massive power plants: There is a major plant five miles to the east of your house, and another major plant five miles to the west, but you have no electricity at your house. That would not make sense, would it? It would do little good to sit in the dark without power, talking about how wonderful the power is five miles in both directions. Nor does it make sense that we would live between two major "power events"—the resurrection of Christ in the past and the resurrection of our bodies in the future—and yet be powerless in our lives today. You have probably noticed that there are pressures and forces in life that want to drag us down, beat us down, and keep us down. If Scripture teaches that there is spiritual power emanating from the resurrection of Christ that will undergird our lives and lift us up, we need to know about it—and we need to partake of it.

Experiencing Resurrection *Life* Between Two Resurrection *Events*

It is good news indeed that the Bible introduces us to a present availability of resurrection power that is to affect our day-to-day lives. Here is a simple breakdown of how this works:

1. Jesus's resurrection from the dead in the past is a resurrection *event.*
2. The receiving of our glorified bodies in the future will be a resurrection *event.*
3. God designed our life in between these two events—our life in the here and now—to be a *process* that is dynamically affected by the power of Jesus' resurrection in the past and by the promised resurrection in our future. We are to live dynamically in the redemptive benefits and power of the Holy Spirit flowing to us from Christ's resurrection in the past. We are also to live purposefully in the hope and strength that comes to us from our future resurrection.

What does this look like practically? Most believers know that forgiveness and the new birth is available to them through the death and resurrection of Jesus, but what if Jesus' resurrection releases much more to us? Imagine the power flowing from Christ's resurrection lifting *our attitudes.* Imagine it lifting our love-walk—the way we treat and interact with others. What about our morals? Our marriages and families? Even our sense of generosity—all transformed and lifted by the power of the resurrection? How about the way we talk—our speech? And what about what we do with our bodies? All of these decisions and actions are meant to be affected by the resurrection of Christ and the status that his resurrection bestows upon us. When we allow this transfer of power to happen, we truly will experience *lift*, and our lives will be elevated into higher degrees of godliness and virtue.

We see this past-present-future paradigm vividly illustrated in Paul's life. When he wrote his second letter to the Corinthian Church, he had just endured an enormously difficult time in his ministry. Paul described being under unimaginable pressure and facing intense despair, yet he found strength and deliverance through the power that God's resurrecting nature provides. Paul writes, "Yes, we had the sentence of death in ourselves, that we should not trust in ourselves but in *God who raises the dead*, who delivered us from so great a death, and does deliver us; in whom we trust that He will still deliver us" (2 Cor. 1:9-10, emphasis mine). Notice that Paul references God raising the dead, and then refers to past, present, and future applications. God *did* deliver us (past), God *does* deliver us (present), and God *will* deliver us (future). We can expect the same help from God that the Apostle Paul received because God is no respecter of persons (Acts 10:34).

Even God-followers in the Old Testament experienced lift by having what might be called "a resurrection mindset." Even though the resurrection of Jesus had not yet occurred, these people of faith still recognized God's life-giving, miracle-working nature. The author of Hebrews notes:

> **HEBREWS 11:17-19 (*NLT*)**
> **17 It was by faith that Abraham offered Isaac as a sacrifice when God was testing him. Abraham, who had received God's promises, was ready to sacrifice his only son, Isaac,**
>
> **18 even though God had told him, "Isaac is the son through whom your descendants will be counted."**
>
> **19 Abraham reasoned that if Isaac died, God was able to bring him back to life again. And in a sense, Abraham did receive his son back from the dead.**

In Romans, Paul writes that Abraham became the father of many nations because he "believed in the God who brings the dead back to life and who creates new things out of nothing" (4:17, *NLT*). While this specific story of God asking Abraham to offer his son as a sacrifice is unique, the principle involving faith and trust is transcendent. Anytime God asks us to obey and follow his instructions, we can be sure that his resurrecting power is able to work in our situation.

Examples of *Lift* in Romans

We clearly see a present-day application of resurrection power throughout the New Testament. As you read the following scriptures, note carefully the connection Paul makes between the resurrection of Jesus and its impact on us—and not just on our status as Christians but also on our conduct in life. Through faith in Christ, we not only partake of resurrection life, but we are also to demonstrate a resurrection lifestyle. Romans 6:4 reads, "We were buried with him through baptism into death, that *just as Christ was raised from the dead* by the glory of the Father, *even so we also should walk in newness of life*" (emphasis mine).

Jesus identified with us in our death so that we could identify with him in his resurrection. If we identify with Christ, then "the glory of the Father" is to affect how we live our everyday lives. We know that resurrection power is to influence our lifestyle in the here and now because Romans 6:13 admonishes us, "Do not present your members as instruments of unrighteousness to sin, but present yourselves to God *as being alive from the dead*, and your members as instruments of righteousness to God" (emphasis mine).

Notice, we are not only to "walk in newness of life" (Rom. 6:4), but we are also to recognize that we are "alive from the dead" (6:13). What we then do with our members—our bodies—should reflect *our* resurrection life status.

Two chapters later, Paul again talks about our partaking of resurrection power:

ROMANS 8:11 (*NLT*)

11 The Spirit of God, who raised Jesus from the dead, lives in you. And just as God raised Christ Jesus from the dead, he will give life to your mortal bodies by this same Spirit living within you.

While it is entirely true that there will be a future work of resurrection when we receive our glorified bodies, it is also true that not all of God's resurrection work toward us is reserved exclusively for the future. The Spirit who raised Jesus from the dead lives in us *now*, and he is certainly not dormant!

Famed theologian and Protestant reformer John Calvin did not believe that Romans 8:11 referred to the final resurrection "but [to] the continued working of the Spirit, by which he gradually mortifies the relics of the flesh and renews in us a celestial life."[8] Calvin certainly believed in the future resurrection, but he thought this specific verse referred to an ongoing, current experience in the life of the believer whereby the Spirit of God empowers us to rise above the pull of the flesh and to receive impartations of heavenly strength. If Calvin is correct here, and I believe that he is, it would be correct to say, "God, I know that you will someday resurrect and completely transform my body, but in the meantime, I believe the Holy Spirit—the one who raised Jesus from the dead—is quickening, energizing, vivifying, and giving life to my mortal body even now!"

The Apostle Paul supports this type of declaration when he writes, "We have the Holy Spirit within us as a foretaste of future glory" (Rom 8:23, *NLT*). Hebrews 6:5 references mature believers as those who have "have tasted the good word of God and the powers of the age to come." What a tremendous thought! Even now, we can sample a taste of the powers of the age to come. In the future, we will receive brand new, glorified,

---

[8] John Calvin, *Commentary on Romans* (Grand Rapids: Christian Classics Ethereal Library, 1539), loc. 458, Kindle.

and resurrected bodies, but right now we have available to us (and should enjoy) this foretaste of future glory, this first taste of heaven.

This idea of experiencing a taste of heaven reminds me Fanny Crosby's great hymn "Blessed Assurance[9]":

Blessed assurance, Jesus is mine

O what a foretaste of glory divine

Heir of salvation, purchase of God

Born of His Spirit, washed in His blood

Yes, heaven will be wonderful for the believer, and receiving our glorified bodies will be a tremendous event, but we do not have to wait for those *events* before we begin the *process* of experiencing God's powerful lift in our daily lives. The Spirit who raised Jesus from the dead is living and operative in us now!

Examples of *Lift* in Ephesians

Similar to those in the Book of Romans, there are teachings in the first chapter of Ephesians about believers experiencing lift through resurrection power. Consider Paul's prayer:

EPHESIANS 1:19-20 (*NLT*)

19 I also pray that you will understand the incredible greatness of God's power for us who believe him. This is the same mighty power

20 that raised Christ from the dead and seated him in the place of honor at God's right hand in the heavenly realms.

[9] Frances J. Crosby, *Blessed Assurance* (Public Domain, 1873).

The *Amplifed Bible* emphasizes the fact that resurrection power is to work *in us* and *for us*! It refers to "the immeasurable and unlimited and surpassing greatness of *His power in and for us who believe*, as demonstrated in the working of His mighty strength, which he exerted in Christ when He raised him from the dead and seated him at his [own] right hand" (emphasis mine). We can know the same power that raised Jesus from the dead in an experiential way!

Greek scholar Kenneth Wuest points out that this incredibly great power that God releases toward us "is not thought of here as operating only in the future, but also at present."[10] Referring to this same passage in Ephesians, Elmer Towns writes:

> If Christians understood and applied the resurrection and ascension of Christ, it would radically change much of the work done for God by them. Christians need not be defeated. The same power that raised Jesus from the dead works not only to save us but to assist us in our Christian life and service.[11]

Yet another commentator states, "God's energetic power which resurrected and exalted Christ in the past is the same power available to believers in the present. What an amazing source of spiritual vitality, power, and strength for living the Christian life!"[12] The Apostle Paul continues and expands this thought of our partaking of Christ's resurrection power later in Ephesians when he writes that God "raised us from the dead along

---

[10] Kenneth S. Wuest, *Word Studies from the Greek New Testament: For the English Reader* (Grand Rapids: Eerdmans, 1997), Logos Bible Software.

[11] Elmer L. Towns, *What The Faith Is All About: Basic Doctrines of Christianity* (Orlando, FL: Harcourt Brace, 1998), 201.

[12] Harold W. Hoehner, *"Ephesians,"* The Bible Knowledge Commentary: An Exposition of the Scriptures. Ed. J. F. Walvoord and R. B. Zuck. Vol. 2. (Wheaton, IL: Victor Books, 1985), 621.

with Christ and seated us with him in the heavenly realms because we are united with Christ Jesus" (Eph. 2:6, *NLT*). Now *that* is *lift*!

Scholars Guy Duffield and Nathaniel Van Cleave refer to resurrection power as "the power that defeated death." They then state that for us who believe, this same power "is sufficient for every day and every emergency."[13] Do we believe that? Do we expect resurrection power to be actively at work in our lives? In *Practice Resurrection*, Eugene Peterson writes, "The resurrection of Jesus establishes the conditions in which we live and mature in the Christian life."[14] Addressing the growth, development, and formation that result from the work of the Holy Spirit in our lives, Peterson continues:

> When we practice resurrection, we continuously enter into what is more than we are. When we practice resurrection, we keep company with Jesus, alive and present, who knows where we are going better than we do, which is always "from glory unto glory."[15]

These are amazing concepts! And all of them point to the same fact—that there is a degree of resurrection power available to us now. No, it is not the full expression that will ultimately be released at Christ's return, resulting in us having fully glorified bodies, but it is certainly enough for us to sense significant spiritual lift and to experience an elevated life. It is enough to provide us encouragement, confidence, peace, and victory in the midst of a world that exerts so much downward pressure on people.

---

[13] Guy P. Duffield and Nathaniel M. Van Cleave, *Foundations for Pentecostal Theology* (Los Angeles: LIFE Bible College, 1987), 202.

[14] Eugene Peterson, *Practice Resurrection: A Conversation of Growing Up in Christ* (Grand Rapids: Eerdman's, 2010), loc. 130, Kindle.

[15] Ibid., loc. 135.

Examples of *Lift* in Philippians

When Paul wrote the precious believers in Philippi, he was feeling the effects of extended hardships and the drain of arduous ministry. He had been beaten and whipped on multiple occasions and shipwrecked four times, and he was experiencing imprisonment for the sake of the gospel. In the first chapter of Philippians, Paul relates the fact that the prospect of heaven had become very attractive to him, but he also expresses his resolve to continue his ministry for the sake of promoting the Philippians' spiritual advancement (Phil. 1:21-26).

In the third chapter of Philippians, Paul makes some dynamic statements regarding the resurrection. No doubt, he still has in mind the ultimate resurrection when believers will receive glorified bodies. However, it appears that there is a distinct awareness in Paul's mind that resurrection power is not exclusively restricted to that wonderful future event. For example, in Philippians 3:10, Paul expresses his desire "that [he] may know [Christ] and the power of his resurrection." The word "know" that Paul uses here does not mean mere cognitive recognition, but it refers to a personal, intimate, and experiential knowledge.

The *Amplified Bible's* rendering of Philippians 3:10 is very powerful in expressing Paul's desire to walk in the updraft—the very lift of God's resurrection power:

PHILIPPIANS 3:10 (*AMP*, EMPHASIS MINE)
10 [For my determined purpose is] that I may know him [that I may progressively become more deeply and intimately acquainted with him, perceiving and recognizing and understanding the wonders of his person more strongly and more clearly], and that I may in *that same way come to know the power outflowing from his resurrection [which it exerts over believers]*.

I have emphasized the last phrase in this verse because I want you to notice that beyond Paul's interest in experiencing the *power* of Christ's resurrection in his life, he also yearns to know more deeply the *person* of Christ himself. We are not seeking power in the misguided, corrupted way that Simon did in Acts 8:9-24. With sincere and humble hearts, we desire to know Christ in ever-increasing measure and to receive the power out-flowing from his resurrection.

Paul continues his thought in the next verse. He writes, "That if possible I may attain to the [spiritual and moral] resurrection [that lifts me] out from among the dead [even while in the body]" (Phil. 3:11, *AMP*). The *Amplified* places an emphasis on Paul's experiencing a here-and-now lift due to the resurrecting power of God. One commentator, however, presents the possibility of an "*either* the future *or* the present" application of Paul's statement. Gregory Sapaugh writes:

> Paul is either looking forward to his own *resurrection* at the Rapture of the church and thus his subsequent triumphant stand before his Lord at the Judgment Seat of Christ, or, with Christ as his pattern, he wants to experience his resurrection power in this life now.[16]

Regardless of whether a person sees Philippians 3:11 as focused entirely on a future physical resurrection or believes that it includes the idea of a "spiritual and moral resurrection" that can provide lift for our lives right now, there are numerous other scriptures to support a "both/and" application instead of an "either/or." It is true that we are awaiting a future resurrection of our bodies, and in the meantime, God's lifting power is available to help us also live a victorious, godly life.

---

[16] Gregory P. Sapaugh, Gregory P, *The Epistle of Paul the Apostle to the Philippians*, The Grace New Testament Commentary. Ed. Robert N. Wilkin (Denton, TX: Grace Evangelical Society, 2010), 904.

A New Way To See Ourselves

We should not see our current location between Jesus' resurrection and our future resurrection as a barren, bereft place. Rather, we should acknowledge that resurrection life vibrantly flows in us because the Resurrecting One and the Resurrected One are living in us now! Paul reminded the Colossians of the Lord's presence in their lives when he said, "Christ in you, the hope of glory" (Col. 1:27). Christ, who indwells the believer through his Spirit, is the one who says, "I am the resurrection and the life" (John 11:25).

Remember also Paul's statement in Romans 8:11: "If the Spirit of Him who raised Jesus from the dead dwells in you, he who raised Christ from the dead will also give life to your mortal bodies through his Spirit who dwells in you." Not only does the Spirit of God dwell in us, Scripture says that our bodies are his very temple (1 Cor. 6:19)! How could he live in us and not affect and influence our life? How could he dwell within us without lifting us? No wonder John said, "You are of God, little children, and have overcome them, because he who is in you is greater than he who is in the world" (1 John 4:4).

Experience *Lift* in Daily Life

What does "lift" look like when it is operating in our lives? When we have yielded to the power that flows from the resurrection of Jesus Christ, we may be surprised at how pervasive and practical God's influence in our lives can be. Resurrection power can drastically affect our overall attitude toward life and our attitude toward others. We can see hope where others see none. We envision possibilities when others have given up. Encouragement rises inside us even in the midst of discouraging circumstances. We reject pessimism, cynicism, and fatalism. We are empowered by a confidence that does not come from this world. Resurrection life provides a wellspring of joy and peace from which we draw and by which we are sustained. We don't see the end of this temporal, mortal existence as the end of life. Rather, we have an eternal perspective of our own lives and of life itself. Everything and everyone takes on greater value because of how and why God created us. "Resurrection" is not just a past event or a future promise; it affects us dynamically in the here and now.

A Resurrection Declaration

Lord, your Word admonishes me to taste and see that you are good, and it is my desire to do so. Jesus, you are the Resurrection and the Life, and I thank you for making yourself real to me. As I come to know you more, I believe that your resurrecting nature and power will influence my life in every way. I thank you, Jesus, for your resurrection, and I also thank you for the future resurrection that your Word promises; I look forward to the day when my body will be transformed and glorified. But I also thank you for the resurrection life that you have called me to experience and benefit from even now. I submit myself, in the entirety of my being to you, and I pray that my attitude, my dealings with others, my speech, and my conduct will all be dynamically affected by the power of your resurrection. Thank you for helping me to walk at a higher level of godliness than I have ever walked before. Help me to walk in the newness of life. I believe that the very same Spirit who raised Jesus from the dead lives in me. He is not only my first taste of heaven, but he also quickens and gives life to my mortal body. Thank you, heavenly Father, for making it real to me that I have been raised with Christ and have been made to sit with him in heavenly places. Like Paul, I want to perceive, recognize, and understand the wonders of Christ's person more strongly and more clearly and come to know the power outflowing from his resurrection. I thank you that both the Resurrected One and the Resurrecting One are in me now, and I set my heart to yielding to your influence in every area of my life. In Jesus' name, I pray—amen.

Bonus Quotes

"Before the Resurrection of Christ, the Holy Spirit came upon individuals only on certain occasions for special tasks. But now, after the Resurrection, Christ through the Holy Spirit dwells in the heart of every believer to give us supernatural power in living our daily lives."

—Billy Graham

"The most casual reader of the New Testament can scarcely fail to see the commanding position the resurrection of Christ holds in Christianity. It is the creator of its new and brighter hopes, of its richer and stronger faith, of its deeper and more exalted experience."

—E. M. Bounds

"The risen life of Jesus is the nourishment and strengthening and blessing and life of a Christian. Our daily experience ought to be that there comes, wavelet by wavelet, that silent, gentle, and yet omnipotent influx into our empty hearts, this very life of Christ Himself."

—Alexander MacLaren

"Doctrines about the Spirit are necessary and inevitable, but the all-important question is not what we mentally believe, but what we experimentally enjoy."

—Donald Gee

"Christ is not a reservoir but a spring. His life is continual, active and ever passing on with an outflow as necessary as its inflow. If we do not perpetually draw the fresh supply from the living Fountain, we shall either grow stagnant or empty. It is, therefore, not so much a perpetual fullness as a perpetual filling."

—A. B. Simpson

Lyrics that Lift: Hymns of the Resurrection

From "The Strife is O'er, the Battle Done" (12th Century Latin)

The strife is o'er, the battle done;

The victory of life is won;

The song of triumph has begun: Alleluia!

The powers of death have done their worst;

But Christ their legions hath dispersed;

Let shouts of holy joy outburst: Alleluia!

The three sad days are quickly sped;

He rises glorious from the dead;

All glory to our risen Head! Alleluia!

He closed the yawning gates of hell;

The bars from heaven's high portals fell;

Let hymns of praise His triumphs tell! Alleluia!

Lord, by the stripes which wounded Thee,

From death's dread sting Thy servants free,

That we may live, and sing to Thee: Alleluia!

 Questions for Reflection and Discussion

1. Before you began reading this book, how often did you think about experiencing resurrection power in your day-to-day life? Did you consider that the resurrection could significantly influence in your daily life?
2. What potential difference would it make in our lives if we no longer saw the resurrection as only a past or future event but recognized that Jesus *is* the Resurrection and the Life?
3. According to the various scriptures in Romans, Ephesians, and Philippians, how much influence can resurrection power have in our day-to-day lives? Can you cite any examples of how the power flowing from Jesus' resurrection has changed your life? In what ways will these various passages of Scripture make you more mindful of yielding to resurrection life, and how might your daily life be different as you tap into more of God's power?
4. In "Blessed Assurance," Fanny Crosby wrote of experiencing "a foretaste of glory divine." What does that mean to you, and to what degree can the Christian actually experience this? Similarly, Hebrews 6:5 speaks of tasting "the powers of the age to come." How much has this concept been a reality in your life, and can you think of ways you could experience this "foretaste of heaven" in greater depth?
5. Based on Second Timothy 2:16-18, what would you say to people if they claimed that the resurrection of the dead has already taken place?
6. Think back through the teaching in this chapter regarding resurrection power in the here and now. List one thing you learned and one thing

you can do right now that will allow you to begin accessing more of God's resurrection power—his *lift*—in your life.

CHAPTER THREE

Off With the Old— On With the New

Yesterday I was crucified with him; today I am glorified with him;

Yesterday I died with him; today I am quickened with him;

Yesterday I was buried with him; today I rise with him.

—Gregory the Theologian, Fourth Century Archbishop of Constantinople

In the previous chapter, we looked at Philippians 3:11 where Paul speaks of his desire to attain the spiritual and moral resurrection that would lift him out from among the dead *even while he was in his body*. We know that God provides power to strengthen, sanctify, and encourage us during our present life. We are in the world, but not of it (John 17:14,16), so it makes sense that God would provide power from heaven for us to live by. We are citizens of heaven (Phil. 3:20), and while we are clearly not *physically* in heaven yet, God's own Presence is active in our lives now, empowering us to live for his glory on the earth.

We also studied Philippians 3:10, where Paul expresses a desire to know Christ and the power of his resurrection. However, there is an important part of this passage that we did not address in the previous chapter. Let's look more closely at the context of Paul's words:

PHILIPPIANS 3:10-11

10 that I may know him and the power of his resurrection, and the fellowship of his sufferings, being conformed to his death,

11 if, by any means, I may attain to the resurrection from the dead.

It is easy to be selective when we read Scripture and only focus on the parts that we like—the parts that are soothing and make us comfortable. We can all be happy about the idea of knowing Jesus better, and of course, we want to know the lift the comes from him—that resurrection power that blesses us now, and the ultimate, future resurrection when we will obtain our new and glorified bodies.

But Paul said something else here that is part of the whole package. In addition to knowing Jesus and the power of his resurrection, Paul also says he wants to know "the fellowship of his sufferings, being conformed to his death." It really is a package deal. If Jesus is truly our Lord, we cannot arbitrarily choose which parts of the Bible to accept and which parts to ignore. The act of fellowshipping in Christ's sufferings and conforming to his death may sound morbid, but it is not. This action goes hand in hand with knowing him and experiencing the power of his resurrection.

It is important here to examine exactly what it means to share in Christ's sufferings. Earlier in this same epistle, Paul describes the basis of Christ's sufferings: "He humbled Himself and became obedient to the point of death, even the death of the cross" (Phil. 2:8). Jesus had already said, "If anyone desires to come after me, let him deny himself, and take up his cross daily, and follow me" (Luke 9:23). Based on these two verses, we get the idea that sharing in Christ's sufferings at least involves humility, obedience, self-denial, and daily discipline. It does not mean that we will be crucified on a cross outside of Jerusalem for the sins of the world; Jesus did this already as our substitute. But the way Jesus lived his life is our example, and we do apply the *principle* of the cross as we walk with God.

Abiding by this principle means that we submit our will to the will of God, as Jesus did when he prayed, "Not my will, but yours, be done" (Luke 22:42). It means we follow Jesus' example in seeking the welfare of others. Romans 15:2-3 instructs us, "Let each of us please his neighbor for his good, leading to edification." Another way we are conformed to the death of Christ is in resisting temptation as he did. He said an emphatic *no* to the world, the flesh, and devil! The author of Hebrews says that Jesus "offered prayers and pleadings, with a loud cry and tears, to the one who could rescue him from death. And God heard his prayers because of his deep reverence for God. Even though Jesus was God's Son, he learned obedience from the things he suffered" (Heb 5:7-8, *NLT*). Jesus did not take obedience unto his Father lightly; he was obedient even to the point of death. God's plan is for us to be committed to fulfilling his will, just as Jesus was, and to die to the thought that our primary goal in life is the gratification of our ego or our flesh.

Paul not only talked about knowing the fellowship of Christ's sufferings, but he also spoke of "being conformed to his death" (Phil. 2:10). Stop and think about the kind of death that Jesus experienced. Romans 6:10 teaches, "For the death that he died, he died to sin once for all; but the life that he lives, he lives to God." It makes sense that if we are conformed to Jesus' death that we, too, will die to sin—we will turn our back on, renounce, and walk away from anything that is displeasing to God and contrary to his Word.

Let me give you an example of what "dying to sin" looks like in the life of a believer. Paul tells believers in Colossae to put some things to death: "So put to death the sinful, earthly things lurking within you. Have nothing to do with sexual immorality, impurity, lust, and evil desires. Don't be greedy, for a greedy person is an idolater, worshiping the things of this world" (Col 3:5, *NLT*). This verse explains that the *old* nature needs to be put to death, and a few verses later, Paul explains that believers are to put on their *new* nature. Off with the old and on with the new leads us to resurrection living!

God will help us "die" to the wrong things so we can "live" to the right things—this is what it means to live a resurrected life. For example, a person who has perpetually complained can discontinue that behavior and instead embrace an attitude of thankfulness and gratitude. Having and living a new life in Christ radically affects our focus. Paul reveals this changed focus in a tremendous statement to the Christians in Colossae:

COLOSSIANS 3:1-3 (*AMP*)

1 If then you have been raised with Christ [to a new life, thus sharing his resurrection from the dead], aim at and seek the [rich, eternal treasures] that are above, where Christ is, seated at the right hand of God.

2 And set your minds and keep them set on what is above (the higher things), not on the things that are on the earth.

3 For [as far as this world is concerned] you have died, and your [new, real] life is hidden with Christ in God.

Verse one in *The Message* reads, "So if you're serious about living this new resurrection life with Christ, *act* like it. Pursue the things over which

Christ presides." God has called us to live resurrection lives *now*, while we are in this mortal body! Another place where believers are told they must choose between death and life is in Romans chapter 8. Paul writes, "For if you live according to the flesh you will die; but if by the Spirit you put to death the deeds of the body, you will live" (v. 13). Douglas Moo describes this "putting to death the deeds of the body" as follows:

> While the Christian is made responsible for this "mortification" of sins, he or she accomplishes this only "through the Spirit." Holiness of life, then, is achieved neither by our own unaided effort—the error of "moralism" or "legalism"—nor by the Spirit apart from our participation—as some who insist that the key to holy living is "surrender" or "let go and let God" would have it—but by our constant living out the "life" placed within us by the Spirit who has taken up residence within. We face here another finely nuanced balance that must not be tipped too far in one direction or the other. Human activity in the process of sanctification is clearly necessary; but that activity is never apart from, nor finally distinct from, the activity of God's Spirit.[17]

We are not to let unrenewed thinking or the lusts of the flesh govern our lives. In Romans 12:1, Paul admonishes believers to present their "bodies a living sacrifice, holy, acceptable to God." He also describes the lusts of the flesh to the Galatian believers, and it is not a pretty list. It includes "sexual immorality, impurity, lustful pleasures, idolatry, sorcery, hostility, quarreling, jealousy, outbursts of anger, selfish ambition, dissension, division, envy, drunkenness, wild parties, and other sins like these" (Gal. 5:19-21, *NLT*). But Paul writes, "Walk in the Spirit, and you shall not fulfill the lust of the flesh," and proceeds to say, "those who are Christ's

---

[17] Douglas J. Moo, *The Epistle to the Romans*, The New International Commentary on the New Testament (Grand Rapids, MI: Eerdmans Publishing, 1996), 495–496.

have crucified the flesh with its passions and desires" (Gal. 5:16, 24). Missionary and theologian E. Stanley Jones explains how to achieve the focus necessary to present our body a living sacrifice. He writes, "I don't fight sin. I expel it by preoccupation with the Higher. Looking at him I am spoiled for anything else."

Remember, also, what Paul taught the Romans: "If by the Spirit you put to death the deeds of the body, you will live" (Rom. 8:13). I do not see in Scripture where Paul told believers to overcome sin by mere will power. I do not see where he told them to do it merely in their own strength or by their own effort. Paul told them that they needed to put the deeds of the body to death *by the Spirit*. In other words, we rely upon the empowerment and enablement of the Spirit of God to help us say *yes* to the right things and *no* to the wrong things. We have a part to play, but we do not accomplish the task without God's aid and assistance.

There is another section of Scripture where this death/life contrast is very evident. Like Jesus, Paul lived a life in which he humbled himself and was obedient to the Father's plan. He certainly did not live to gratify himself or indulge his carnal nature. In fact, Paul's obedience to God often put him in situations where his flesh would have been most uncomfortable. But it was in this realm of deliberate, unwavering obedience to God where Paul found that he could not trust in his own strength "but in God who raises the dead" (2 Cor. 1:9). In the verses that follow, Paul describes horrific pressures that he faced, things that could have brought great discouragement and distress into his life. But as these negative elements worked against Paul, a greater power was working on his behalf. He calls it "resurrection life."

2 CORINTHIANS 4:7-11 (*AMP*)

7 However, we possess this precious treasure [the divine Light of the Gospel] in [frail, human] vessels of earth, that the grandeur and exceeding greatness of the power may be shown to be from God and not from ourselves.

8 We are hedged in (pressed) on every side [troubled and oppressed in every way], but not cramped or crushed; we suffer embarrassments and are perplexed and unable to find a way out, but not driven to despair;

9 We are pursued (persecuted and hard driven), but not deserted [to stand alone]; we are struck down to the ground, but never struck out and destroyed;

10 Always carrying about in the body the liability and exposure to the same putting to death that the Lord Jesus suffered, so that the [resurrection] life of Jesus also may be shown forth by and in our bodies.

11 For we who live are constantly [experiencing] being handed over to death for Jesus' sake, that the [resurrection] life of Jesus also may be evidenced through our flesh which is liable to death.

The resurrection life that Paul describes here is not a reference to his getting a new, glorified body in the future. Paul is expounding on how God *lifted* him—gave him resurrection life—when all the forces of hell were trying to discourage, deter, and destroy him.

Remember, Paul states in Philippians 3:10 that he wants to know Christ and the power of his resurrection, but he also wants to know the fellowship of his sufferings and to be conformed to his death. Again—this is really a package deal. If you indulge your fleshly, carnal nature and live for ego, selfish ambition, and personal gain, you will not get to know Christ that way, and you certainly will not partake of and benefit from resurrection power in your everyday life. However, if you embrace the whole counsel of God and seek to follow him with all of your heart, you will be empowered as you humbly obey God and take up your cross daily. You will come to know Christ and his resurrection power. Embracing Christ's sufferings and being conformed to his death is not a morbid or grim proposition. Death to the wrong things is part of moving into resurrection life, which enables us to enjoy the right things. I love Paul's words:

ROMANS 8:15 (*MSG*)

15 "This resurrection life you received from God is not a timid, grave-tending life. It's adventurously expectant, greeting God with a childlike 'What's next, Papa?'"

Understanding the future resurrection of our bodies creates hope for the future, and that is wonderful. But understanding the resurrection life that is available right now enables us to approach every day with enthusiasm and expectancy about what God can do in us and through us in the here and now.

A Resurrection Declaration

Lord, thank you for granting me citizenship in heaven, even before I arrive there. I also thank you that your very presence is in me *now*, strengthening me and helping me live in this present world. Thank you for helping me to know you, and the power of your resurrection, and even the fellowship of your sufferings. Help me say *yes* to the right things and *no* to the wrong things. Help me die to the things that Jesus died to, so that I can live more fully to all the good things that you have for me. Help me live in obedience to all of God's will and to decline things detrimental to my life and contrary to your will. Like Jesus, I pray, "Not my will, but your will be done." Help me put to death all of the things that are not a part of the resurrection life you have called me to live, and since I've been raised with Christ, help me to seek the things that are above—the higher things of life. Thank you for helping me—by your Spirit—to put to death the things of sinful flesh. Thank you for helping me renew my mind to your Word and present my body to you as a living sacrifice, holy and acceptable to you. I believe that the resurrection life of Jesus can and will be demonstrated in and through my body. I believe my body is a vessel through which God will work and glorify himself. Though it will someday die, it will also be resurrected. In the meantime, I will glorify God through my body. In Jesus' name, I pray—amen.

Bonus Quotes

"Remember that He who rose from the dead, rose to pour out His Holy Spirit into human lives, and, by that Spirit, to make available to any individual all the fullness of Himself, twenty-four hours a day."

—Ray C. Stedman

"God has defeated Satan through the death and resurrection of the Lord Jesus Christ. Through this overwhelming victory, God has also empowered you to overcome any temptation to sin and has provided sufficient resources for you to respond biblically to any problem of life. By relying on God's power and being obedient to His Word, you can be an overcomer in any situation."

—John C. Broger

"In his life, Christ is an example, showing us how to live; in his death, he is a sacrifice, satisfying our sins; in his resurrection, a conqueror; in his ascension, a king; in his intercession, a high priest."

—Martin Luther

"God wants the whole person and He will not rest till He gets us in entirety. No part of the man will do."

—A. W. Tozer

"Christ and his benefits go inseparably and undividedly… Many would willingly receive his privileges, who will not receive his person; but it cannot be; if we will have one, we must take the other too: Yea, we must accept his person first, and then his benefits: as it is in the marriage covenant, so it is here."

—John Flavel

 Lyrics that Lift: Hymns of the Resurrection

From "Welcome Happy Morning! Age to Age Shall Say" by Venantius Fortunatus (6th Century)

Author and sustainer,
Source of life and breath;
You for our salvation
Trod the path of death:

Jesus Christ is living,
God for evermore!
Now let all creation
Hail him and adore.

Loose our souls imprisoned,
Bound with Satan's chain;
All that now is fallen,
Raise to life again!

Show your face in brightness,
Shine the whole world through;
Hope returns with daybreak,
Life returns with you.

Questions for Reflection and Discussion

1. In Philippians 3:10, Paul says he wants to know "the fellowship of [Christ's] sufferings, being conformed to His death." How does this principle apply to the believer? In what way(s) can we emulate Christ's suffering? What types of things might a Christian "die to" that would be necessary to experiencing resurrection power in daily life?

2. Consider the following statement from this chapter: "God will help us die to the wrong things so we can live a resurrected life toward the right things." Can you cite any examples of how you've seen this principle work in your life?

3. Review Douglas Moo's statement regarding Romans 8:13 on page 47. He mentions two different extremes of believers' dealings with sin. What happens when a Christian views overcoming sin as entirely God's responsibility, and what happens when a Christian thinks he has to do it all in his own strength? How well do you think you've established "the blend" of trusting in God's power to help you while also cooperating through your beliefs, thinking, and actions?

4. Review the Bonus Quotes by Ray C. Stedman and John C. Broger. They communicate an awareness of, a reliance upon, and a drawing from resurrection life and resurrection power "twenty-four hours a day" and "in any situation." What can you do to make yourself more aware of this available help? What can you do to partake of it on a regular basis?

5. Romans 8:15 in *The Message* associates a joyful, childlike expectation with the resurrection life that is to be enjoyed by the believer. To what

degree do you have that kind of positive anticipation regarding your life in Christ?

6. Think back through the teaching in this chapter regarding putting off the old nature and putting on the new. List one thing you learned and one thing you can do right now that will allow you to begin accessing more of God's resurrection power—his *lift*—in your life.

SECTION II

How Lift Operated in the Lives of Bible Characters

CHAPTER FOUR

The Upward Call: *Lift* in the Life of Paul

I'll go anywhere as long as it's forward.

—David Livingstone

If anyone ever needed *lift*, it was Paul. His résumé of resilience is almost beyond imagination. To make it through what he experienced and still be full of determination and resolve is nothing short of supernatural. Consider Paul's own synopsis of what he experienced in his life and ministry (2 Cor. 11:23-25, *NLT*):

- Imprisoned frequently
- Whipped too many times to count
- Repeatedly threatened with imminent death
- Received 39 lashes—5 different times
- Beaten with rods 3 times

- Shipwrecked 3 times (and then again in Acts 27)
- Suffered a night and day adrift at sea

If all of that isn't enough, Paul proceeds to explain more that he endured:

2 CORINTHIANS 11:26-27 (*NLT*)

26 I have traveled on many long journeys. I have faced danger from rivers and from robbers. I have faced danger from my own people, the Jews, as well as from the Gentiles. I have faced danger in the cities, in the deserts, and on the seas. And I have faced danger from men who claim to be believers but are not.

27 I have worked hard and long, enduring many sleepless nights. I have been hungry and thirsty and have often gone without food. I have shivered in the cold, without enough clothing to keep me warm.

Earlier in the same epistle, Paul makes a statement revealing the spiritual lift he experienced from God's presence and power operating in his life. He states, "Even though our outward man is perishing, yet the inward man is being renewed day by day" (2 Cor. 4:16). *The Message* renders this same verse, "Even though on the outside it often looks like things are falling apart on us, on the inside, where God is making new life, not a day goes by without his unfolding grace." When I hear of someone thriving and prevailing in the midst of the type of pressures Paul experienced, I want to know what his secret is. I want to learn how to tap into the same sense of lift and empowerment that he experienced.

Prior to meeting Jesus, Paul lived a very *religious* life. After his encounter with the Lord on the road to Damascus (Acts 9:3-19), Paul began living a *resurrection* life. The difference between a religious life and a resurrection life is huge. People can be religious, engaging in all kinds of rituals and observing countless regulations, and yet have no covenant or relationship with the true and living God. Jesus came that we might "have and enjoy life, and have it in abundance (to the full, till it overflows)" (John 10:10, *AMP*). Never settle for a mere religious life when God wants you to enjoy a resurrection life.

With all of this in mind, let's look back at some of the statements that Paul makes in Philippians chapter 3.

> **PHILIPPIANS 3:10-14**
> **10 that I may know him and the power of his resurrection, and the fellowship of his sufferings, being conformed to his death,**
>
> **11 if, by any means, I may attain to the resurrection from the dead.**
>
> **12 Not that I have already attained, or am already perfected; but I press on, that I may lay hold of that for which Christ Jesus has also laid hold of me.**
>
> **13 Brethren, I do not count myself to have apprehended; but one thing I do, forgetting those things which are behind and reaching forward to those things which are ahead,**
>
> **14 I press toward the goal for the prize of the upward call of God in Christ Jesus.**

We have already addressed Paul's references to the resurrection. We know that many scriptures address a future physical resurrection, but there is a strong likelihood that Paul here is also addressing a right-now resurrection power. This kind of spiritual lift would have strengthened and empowered Paul as he journeyed with God. It seems to me that Paul had already experienced a degree of resurrection power in his life and desired to experience even more lift as he awaited the ultimate resurrection that would take place in the future.

Not Yet Perfect

Paul makes some other powerful statements here. First, he says that he has not already attained, neither is he already perfect (verse 12). Then he says, "I do not count myself to have apprehended" (verse 13). Paul knew that he had room to grow, that there was still progress to be made. Humility is a prerequisite to receiving help from God! You will never experience lift in your life if you think you've already reached the pinnacle of growth and achievement. Why would you trust God for advancement, promotion, and progress if you have already arrived? Why would you press forward? A Christian who understands the progressive nature of spiritual growth can say, "God loves me just the way I am, but he loves me too much to let me stay this way." The same believer can also say, "I am not all that I'm going to be, but thank God I am not what I used to be." Though we are "complete in Christ" (Col, 2:10), we are not necessarily yet completely developed or matured in Christ—we always have room to grow. To think otherwise is to invite complacency into our lives.

Never Go Backward

Paul also said he was "forgetting those things which are behind and reaching forward to those things which are ahead" (Phil. 3:13). Paul's forgetting the past was key to his establishing forward momentum in his life. Paul had some issues in his history that could have been a major hindrance to him. He could have been crippled with guilt over his persecution of believers. For example, he took part in the murder of Stephen, an early Christian preacher (Acts 7:57–8:1). Consider the following verses where Paul (previously known as Saul) describes his pre-conversion activities:

ACTS 8:3 (*MSG*)

3 And Saul just went wild, devastating the church, entering house after house after house, dragging men and women off to jail.

ACTS 22:4 (*NLT*)

4 I persecuted the followers of the Way, hounding some to death, arresting both men and women and throwing them in prison.

ACTS 26:10-11 (*NIV*)

10 I put many of the Lord's people in prison, and when they were put to death, I cast my vote against them.

11 Many a time I went from one synagogue to another to have them punished, and I tried to force them to blaspheme. I was so obsessed with persecuting them that I even hunted them down in foreign cities.

1 TIMOTHY 3:13 (*NLT*)

13 I used to blaspheme the name of Christ. In my insolence, I persecuted his people. But God had mercy on me because I did it in ignorance and unbelief.

In order for Paul to move *forward with God*, he had to forget his *past without God.* Paul understood that because of God's mercy, he had been forgiven. However, Paul had to forgive himself. He had to let go of what was behind him so he could reach forward to what was ahead of him. Gary Chapman writes, "I am amazed by how many individuals mess up every new day with yesterday. They insist on bringing into today the failures of yesterday and in so doing, they pollute a potentially wonderful day."[18]

An astute reader might recognize that while Paul said he was forgetting the past, he actually referenced it periodically throughout the Book

---

[18] Gary Chapman, *The Five Love Languages: The Secret to Love That Lasts* (Chicago: Northfield Publishing, 2010), loc. 610, Kindle.

of Acts and in his epistles. His past was part of his testimony. What is important to recognize is that "forgetting" in the biblical sense does not refer to amnesia. Forgetting is not the inability to recall what has happened in the past. Rather, forgetting in the biblical sense is actually a decision not to let the past dominate your life, define your identity, or dictate your future. This is why Paul could talk about his history as a persecutor of the Church without being in bondage to guilt or condemnation. Spiritually, he was free from the grip of the past because he understood that the blood of Jesus had cleansed him from all sin, and he could actually use his past for the glory of God.

Warren Wiersbe, pastor and biblical commentator, explains the scriptural understanding of forgetting this way:

> Please keep in mind that in Bible terminology, "to forget" does not mean "to fail to remember." Apart from senility, hypnosis, or a brain malfunction, no mature person can forget what has happened in the past. We may wish that we could erase certain bad memories, but we cannot. "To forget" in the Bible means "no longer to be influenced by or affected by." When God promises, "And their sins and iniquities will I remember no more" (Heb. 10:17), He is not suggesting that He will conveniently have a bad memory! This is impossible with God. What God is saying is, "I will no longer hold their sins against them. Their sins can no longer affect their standing with Me or influence My attitude toward them."
>
> So, "forgetting those things which are behind" does not suggest an impossible feat of mental and psychological gymnastics by which we try to erase the sins and mistakes of the past. *It simply means that we break the power of the past by living for the future.*

> We cannot change the past, but we can change the *meaning* of the past. There were things in Paul's past that could have been weights to hold him back (1 Tim. 1:12–17), but they became inspirations to speed him ahead. The events did not change, but his understanding of them changed.[19]

Other commentators provide great insights on these verses as well:

> The word Paul uses means "overlooking." Our past is irrelevant and those things we once relied on now must be discarded, that all our energy might be given to following Christ.[20]

Also:

> *Forgetting those things that are behind.* [Paul] alludes to runners, who do not turn their eyes aside in any direction, lest they should slacken the speed of their course, and, more especially, do not look behind to see how much ground they have gone over, but hasten forward unremittingly towards the goal.[21]

It is also important to recognize that Paul not only needed to forget his past *failures*, but he also had to forget his past *successes*. He could be thankful for the positive things God accomplished through him after his conversion, but he did not allow his accomplishments to make him complacent or lethargic. He did not rest on his laurels, so to speak, and become lazy. He did not sit back and say, "I have done more than my fair share. Now I'm going to relax and let other people carry the load." If the enemy cannot discourage a person through their past failures, he will happily try

---

19 Warren W. Wiersbe, *The Bible Exposition Commentary*. Vol. 2. (Wheaton, IL: Victor Books, 1996), Logos Bible Software.

20 Lawrence O. Richards, *The Bible Reader's Companion* (Wheaton: Victor Books, 1991), Logos Bible Software.

21 John Calvin and John Pringle, *Commentaries on the Epistles of Paul the Apostle to the Philippians, Colossians, and Thessalonians* (Bellingham, WA: Logos Bible Software, 2010).

to lull people into complacency because of their past successes. Paul did not succumb to either temptation. He did not wallow in guilt over past sins, nor did he gloat over previous accomplishments.

Forward and Upward

Paul made it a habit to move forward. Regardless of bad or good things that had happened previously, he continued to move in the direction of progress. Paul also spoke twice of pressing on—of pressing forward—in his journey.

In Philippians 3:12 he states, "I *press* on, that I may lay hold of that for which Christ Jesus has also laid hold of me" (emphasis mine).

Then, in verse 14, he says, "I *press* toward the goal for the prize of the upward call of God in Christ Jesus" (emphasis mine).

Commenting on Philippians 3:12, John Chrysostom said, "Consider how the pursuer strains in his pursuit. He sees nothing, he thrusts away all who impede him with great force, he cherishes his mind, his eye, his strength, his soul and his body, looking at nothing other than the crown."[22] In spite of enormous opposition, Paul continued to put one foot in front of the other. He knew great obstacles lay ahead, but instead of being discouraged or disheartened, he says, "But none of these things move me; nor do I count my life dear to myself, so that I may finish my race with joy" (Acts 20:24). Paul's sense of purpose lifted him and propelled him forward in life.

In aeronautics, thrust and lift work together to make a plane fly. When the thrust and lift of a plane are greater than drag and weight, the plane flies. Where does our lift and thrust come from? I believe it comes from

[22] Edwards, M. J. *Galatians, Ephesians, Philippians.* Downers Grove, IL: InterVarsity Press, 1999. Print. Ancient Christian Commentary on Scripture NT 8.

the power of God—from His Word and Spirit at work in our lives. Where does weight and drag come from? It comes from this world—from the curse of sin that is in the earth, and from the pressures and distractions that come at us from so many directions. The author of Hebrews was not thinking of aeronautics when he wrote, "Let us lay aside every weight, and the sin which so easily ensnares us" (12:1), but he may as well have been. The same weight and sin that will keep us from effectively running our race will also keep us from enjoying the elevated life that God has for us. The point is simple: If we are going to move forward and upward as Paul did, we must let go of the things that are keeping us down and holding us back.

We must also have something toward which to move. Without a sense of purpose, people will coast, drift, and flounder. They end up living life simply reacting to situations and circumstances. People who are committed to a purpose live proactively. They actively pursue divinely implanted goals. In short, they are living the way Paul describes when he states, "I press toward the goal for the prize of the upward call of God in Christ Jesus" (Phil. 3:14). There are four important elements in this verse: Paul refers to 1) pressing, 2) the goal, 3) the prize, and 4) the upward call.

Paul possessed drive and determination. He strenuously exerted himself for a great cause. He was committed to a purpose, and the purpose consumed him. Wiersbe notes that the phrase "I press" was used "to describe a hunter eagerly pursuing his prey."[23] There was determination and intensity in Paul's stride. There was nothing passive about his pursuit of God's will. Paul also says that he was moving toward a goal, that he perceived a prize, and that he was responding to an upward call. The great apostle was deliberate and intentional in his spiritual pursuits.

---

[23] Wiersbe, Warren W. *The Bible Exposition Commentary*. Vol. 2. (Wheaton, IL: Victor Books, 1996), Logos Bible Software.

We, too, must be deliberate and intentional in pursuing God's plan for our life. We must let go of the past—both failures and successes—and not allow anything to sidetrack us from our goal. A. W. Tozer rightly says, "Complacency is a deadly foe of all spiritual growth. Acute desire must be present or there will be no manifestation of Christ to his people."[24] May we, God's people, hunger for and pursue the knowledge of Jesus and his resurrection power so that we can experience the sense of divine lift that comes only from him.

---

[24] A. W. Tozer, *The Pursuit of God* (Christian Miracle Foundation Press, 2011), loc. 175, Kindle.

❗ A Resurrection Declaration

Lord, thank you for the resolve and resilience demonstrated by the Apostle Paul. Help me follow his example in following after you with my whole heart. Like Paul, I recognize that even though the outward man is perishing, the inward man is being renewed day by day. Continually refresh, renew, and rejuvenate me by the working of your Spirit in my inner man. I realize that although you have begun a great work in me, I am not yet perfect nor have I attained complete spiritual maturity. As a result, I continue to hunger for greater knowledge of you and greater spiritual development in my life. I determine to forget the past, to reach forward to the things that are ahead, and to press toward the goal for the prize of the high calling that you have for my life. I believe that the thrust and lift you provide to me by your Spirit will help me rise above the weight and drag that come from this world. As I continue to pursue you and yield to your influence in my life, I know that you will take me forward and upward in my walk with you. In Jesus' name, I pray—amen.

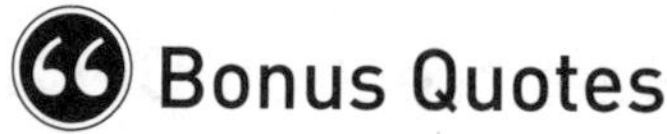

Bonus Quotes

"God commands us to be filled with the Spirit; and if we are not filled, it is because we are living beneath our privileges. I think that is the great trouble with Christendom today: we are not living up on the plane where God would have us live."

—D. L. Moody

"The greatness of a man's power is the measure of his surrender."

—William Booth

"What God expects us to attempt, He also enables us to achieve."

—Stephen Olford

"Sooner or later every believer discovers that the Christian life is a battleground, not a playground."

—D. Martin Lloyd Jones

"Men ought to seek with their whole hearts to be filled with the Spirit of God. Without being filled with the Spirit, it is utterly impossible that an individual Christian or a church can ever live or work as God desires."

– Andrew Murray

Lyrics that Lift: Hymns of the Resurrection

From "One Day" by J. Wilbur Chapman (1908)

One day the grave could conceal Him no longer,
One day the stone rolled away from the door;
Then He arose, over death He had conquered;
Now is ascended, my Lord evermore!

Living, He loved me; dying, He saved me;
Buried, He carried my sins far away;
Rising, He justified freely forever;
One day He's coming—oh, glorious day!

Questions for Reflection and Discussion

1. How would you explain the Apostle Paul's resilience in the face of horrific opposition and persecution? What had he learned about God's grace and God's help, how did he access it, and what results did it produce in his life?

2. How important is it to share in Paul's attitude of "I have not yet arrived; I am not yet perfect"? What does having this attitude allow us to receive and do? If we do not have the same attitude Paul displayed, what will be the likely results in our lives?

3. The Apostle Paul expressed his commitment to "forgetting those things which are behind." How was he able to do this when his actions against others had been so terrible? How successful have you been in forgetting things in your past? Are there areas that need some work?

4. Explain the biblical meaning of "forgetting" according to the definitions and descriptions given in this chapter. How is this different from losing the mental ability to recall the past?

5. In what we might call "spiritual aerodynamics," what creates thrust and lift in your life? What are the sources of weight and drag?

6. Think back through the teaching in this chapter regarding the upward call and *lift* in the life of Paul. List one thing you learned and one thing you can do right now that will allow you to begin accessing more of God's resurrection power—his *lift*—in your life.

CHAPTER FIVE

You Can't Keep a Good Man Down: *Lift* in the Life of Joseph

When my heart is overwhelmed;
Lead me to the rock that is higher than I.

—Psalm 61:2

One of the most remarkable stories in the Old Testament involves Joseph. His life is a testimony to the principle of lift! Betrayals, disappointments, and adversity repeatedly tried to drag Joseph down and destroy him, but there was a divine lift—the favor of God—that caused Joseph to rise back up, and promotion ultimately prevailed in his life. If anyone ever had the right to scream out, "Life is not fair!" it was Joseph. If anyone ever had the right to wallow in self-pity and be resentful of others, it was Joseph. But the hand of God was upon his life, and Joseph's response to the favor of God created what can only be called supernatural buoyancy, and nothing could keep him down.

Though Joseph was loved and favored by his father, he was hated and envied by his older brothers. Unable to deal with their resentment in a positive way, they developed an unthinkable plan: They threw their younger brother into a pit and sold him into slavery. Though Joseph was a victim of his brothers' malice, he refused to adopt a victim mentality. In spite of the betrayal and rejection Joseph experienced, something on the inside of him knew that he had intrinsic dignity and worth that was not determined by the way he had been treated.

Genesis 39:2-4 tells us that "the Lord was with Joseph, and he was a successful man; and he was in the house of his master the Egyptian. And his master saw that the Lord was with him and that the Lord made all he did to prosper in his hand. So Joseph found favor in his sight, and served him. Then he made him overseer of his house, and all that he had he put under his authority."

It may have emotionally devastated Joseph to be treated so despicably by his brothers, but he was not consumed by hurt and pain. Instead, he lived out of the grace of God, and as a result, he experienced lift!

It would be great to think that once a person overcomes a setback, he or she will never face another disappointment, but this is rarely the case. The attacks against Joseph were not over. As he became more prosperous and successful, his boss' wife lied and fabricated false charges against him. Though his conduct was without reproach, Joseph lost his position in the household and was imprisoned. Once again, he had every opportunity to be angry toward God (even though God was certainly not his problem) and could have become full of bitterness against the growing number of people who had done him wrong. Instead, Joseph refused to define himself by the false lies of others and continued acting in a godly manner. He did not sit in his jail cell pouting and feeling sorry for himself, grumbling about how he had been done wrong. Instead, this is what happened:

GENESIS 39:21-23

21 But the Lord was with Joseph and showed him mercy, and he gave him favor in the sight of the keeper of the prison.

22 And the keeper of the prison committed to Joseph's hand all the prisoners who were in the prison; whatever they did there, it was his doing.

23 The keeper of the prison did not look into anything that was under Joseph's authority, because the Lord was with him; and whatever he did, the Lord made it prosper.

Joseph kept his heart right with God and served with excellence. Instead of reflecting the treatment he had received from others, his conduct demonstrated God's favor that was upon his life.

In the process of time, two of Pharaoh's servants were imprisoned, and Joseph—with God's help—accurately interpreted their dreams. When one of those servants was due to be restored to service in the king's household, Joseph asked him to put in a good word for him. However, the official never mentioned Joseph to Pharaoh for two full years. That is a long time to sit in prison because someone forgets about you! Nevertheless, Pharaoh eventually had a dream that needed interpretation, and that is when Joseph's name was finally mentioned. Called to stand before Pharaoh, Joseph—by the ability of God—again interprets a dream. He was then elevated to the position of "Prime Minister" to govern over Egypt.

What a story! Joseph's journey took him from the pit to the prison to the palace. A tremendous sense of lift operated in Joseph's life. When every circumstance tried to drag him down, beat him down, and keep him down, Joseph just kept rising! There was a supernatural resilience operating in his life.

Valuable insight into Joseph's success is revealed later in his life—after he married and had children. In that day, the names of children were often significant, relating to important events and history worth remembering. Joseph gave his first two sons names that indicate the values that were tremendously important to him.

GENESIS 41:51-52 (*NLT*)
51 Joseph named his older son Manasseh, for he said, "God has made me forget all my troubles and everyone in my father's family."

52 Joseph named his second son Ephraim, for he said, "God has made me fruitful in this land of my grief."

"Manasseh" means *to forget*, and "Ephraim" means *to be fruitful.* The order of these names is significant. Just like Paul had to forget those things that were behind him in order to obtain what was ahead of him (Phil. 3:13), Joseph had to forget things from his past in order to move into fruitfulness. *The Message* renders verse 52 as saying, "He named his second son Ephraim (Double Prosperity), saying, 'God has prospered me in the land of my sorrow.'"

One of the most amazing things about Joseph is the role he played in the lives of the family members who betrayed him. Having been elevated to Prime Minister, Joseph coordinated a nationwide food storage program, which not only sustained Egypt during famine but also fed and saved the lives of his brothers and their families. With his position of authority, Joseph could have ordered all of his brothers killed in retribution, but he showed great mercy instead. When his brothers expressed remorse for the way they had treated him, Joseph replies: "You intended to harm me, but

God intended it all for good. He brought me to this position so I could save the lives of many people" (Gen. 50:20, *NLT*). Joseph realized that he was *lifted* so that he could become a *lifter*!

The parallel between Joseph and Paul is interesting. For Joseph to experience fruitfulness, he had to forget things that others had done to him. For Paul to move into the upward call of God, he had to forget things that he had done to others. Both of them experienced lift, and both of them had to put the past behind them to embrace the destiny that was ahead of them. As with Paul, the "forgetting" Joseph refers to is obviously not amnesia or the inability to mentally recall certain historical information. Joseph decided not to allow the past to define his identity, determine his worth, or dictate his future.

I remember hearing a story about Clara Barton, founder of the American Red Cross. Apparently, someone had done her wrong years before, but she moved beyond it. When someone mentioned the situation, she acted oblivious to what was being said. When they asked her if she remembered it, she responded by saying, "No. I distinctly remember forgetting it." Of course, this is a play on words, but forgetting, releasing, and putting the past behind us is imperative if we want to move forward.

When Jacob was about to die, he spoke the following words concerning his son Joseph:

> **GENESIS 49:23-26 (*NIV*)**
> **23 With bitterness archers attacked him; they shot at him with hostility.**
>
> **24 But his bow remained steady, his strong arm stayed limber, because of the hand of the Mighty One of Jacob, because of the Shepherd, the Rock of Israel,**

25 Because of your father's God, who helps you, because of the Almighty, who blesses you with blessings of the skies above, blessings of the deep springs below, blessings of the breast and womb.

26 Your father's blessings are greater than the blessings of the ancient mountains, than the bounty of the age-old hills. Let all these rest on the head of Joseph, on the brow of the prince among his brothers.

This passage tells us that Joseph was mightily blessed. Joseph experienced an elevated life but it wasn't because:

- People were always nice to him—they weren't.
- He always had good circumstances—he didn't.
- People always treated him fairly—they didn't.
- Things always happened quickly for him—they didn't.
- People always told the truth about him—they didn't.
- People remembered him and showed appreciation for him—they didn't.

Despite terrible circumstances and mistreatment, Joseph was elevated by God and lifted by divine favor. Don't think that you are going to live an elevated life because of a lack of opposition. Typically, an elevated life must be lived *in spite* of opposition. Joseph didn't experience lift because he was never knocked down. Rather, lift is what kept elevating him after he was knocked down time and time again.

A major lesson from Joseph's life is that other people can't write your narrative—the story of your life—unless you let them. Other people's decisions and actions certainly affected Joseph, but he believed that God would have the final word, and God absolutely did. As Jacob articulated, Joseph was a target of bitterness and hostility, but he was also the recipient of God's favor and blessings. Joseph chose to let go of what had been unleashed against him and hold fast to the One who was for him, working on his behalf.

If we want to experience lift in life there are important principles to remember. Consider this profound statement:

ISAIAH 54:17 (*NLT*)
17 No weapon turned against you will succeed. You will silence every voice raised up to accuse you. These benefits are enjoyed by the servants of the Lord; their vindication will come from me. I, the Lord, have spoken!

Joseph did not silence the voices raised against him by verbally attacking or retaliating against his adversaries. Instead, he exhibited a response advocated by Peter centuries later. Peter writes, "It is God's will that your honorable lives should silence those ignorant people who make foolish accusations against you" (1 Pet. 2:15, *NLT*).

Over the years, I have interacted with many people who grew up in a negative environment. They were not sold into slavery or thrown into prison on fabricated charges like Joseph was, but neither were they raised in an encouraging, nurturing atmosphere. Some heard words spoken over them that eroded their confidence and self-esteem. Perhaps a parent told them that they would never amount to much, or perhaps a teacher told them that they were not as smart as a sibling. Such words can pierce deeply, bring profound pain, and set limitations on a person's life, but they don't have to be the final authority. We have the final say (as we agree with God) and can rise above the limitations that other people and life in general try to set on us.

The Old Testament provides an example for us to follow. Because of the challenges they faced while journeying through the wilderness, the Israelites allowed doubt and unbelief to fill them with discouragement.

Eventually, they said that it would have been better if they had stayed in Egypt—that they were all going to die in the wilderness, and that their children would perish as well. God's response to their negative murmurings is amazing. He told them that they *would* in fact die, just as they had said over and over. But he had a different plan for their children. God said, "You said your children would be taken as prisoners of war. Instead, I will bring them into the land you rejected, and they will enjoy it" (*GW*).

It is important to remember that other people do not have the final say over your life, especially when God himself has spoken other words—positive words, life-giving words, edifying words—over your life. You can choose to believe and act upon what God has said about you. Peoples' words may tend to drag you down, but God's words will lift you up. That's the great lesson from Joseph's life. Through negative words and actions, other people exerted tremendous downward pressure against Joseph; even though he felt their effects, God's favor transcended and superseded all that came against him. Through perseverance and trust, Joseph saw the fulfillment of what Isaiah had described (Isa. 54:17)—the weapons that were formed against him were not ultimately successful, and his vindication from God was realized.

We may not be called to do exactly what Joseph did, and (thankfully) we may not face the exact kind of hardships he encountered. However, the God that favored him and lifted him is the same God who will favor and lift us.

❗ A Resurrection Declaration

Lord, thank you for Joseph's example. I want to replicate his type of character, steadfastness, and faithfulness in my own life. Your favor helped Joseph overcome so many obstacles and setbacks, and I yield myself to your favor as well. Help me to obey you as Joseph did and to remain committed and consecrated to you no matter what. Thank you for helping me walk in forgiveness as Joseph did, letting go of the hurtful past and moving consistently toward a better, brighter future. I believe that as I am faithful and obedient to you, you will promote and elevate me to a place where I can glorify you and serve others. I believe that you are even now helping me forget the past and move into fruitfulness. I declare the promise of your Word—that no weapon formed against me will prosper, and no matter what others have thought, said, or done against me, you will ultimately cause me to prevail. In Jesus' name, I pray—amen.

Bonus Quotes

"In one bold stroke, forgiveness obliterates the past and permits us to enter the land of new beginnings."

—Billy Graham

"If you are suffering from a bad man's injustice, forgive him lest there be two bad men."

—Augustine

"As a Christian you have to live in the midst of an ungodly world, and it is of little use for you to cry 'Woe is me.' Jesus did not pray "O that you should be taken out of the world," and what He did not pray for you need not desire. Better far in the Lord's strength to meet the difficulty, and glorify Him in it."

—Charles Spurgeon

"In the Kingdom of God, service is not a stepping-stone to nobility: it is nobility, the only kind of nobility that is recognized."

—T. W. Manson

"If God is for us, who can be against us? He who did not spare His own Son, but delivered Him up for us all, how shall He not with Him also freely give us all things?"

—The Apostle Paul (Romans 8:31-32)

Lyrics that Lift: Hymns of the Resurrection

From "Death Hath No Terrors" by Charles P. Jones (1901)

Death hath no terrors for the blood bought one,

O glory hallelujah to the Lamb!

The boasted vict'ry of the grave is gone,

O glory hallelujah to the Lamb!

Jesus rose from the dead,

Rose triumphant as He said,

Snatched the vict'ry from the grave,

Rose again our souls to save—

O glory hallelujah to the Lamb!

 Questions for Reflection and Discussion

1. Joseph experienced repeated disappointments and setbacks in his life. How did Joseph deal with repeated challenges and prolonged periods of difficulty? To what degree have you needed to implement some of these same approaches in your life?

2. God's favor was obviously at work in Joseph's life, but that favor did not automatically remove all of Joseph's problems or immediately place him at the highest position he would achieve. How important was faithfulness and patience in Joseph's life? How important are faithfulness and patience in our lives?

3. Discuss the significance in the naming of Joseph's two sons. How important was the sequence of the two names? In other words, why did "to forget" need to be before "to be fruitful"?

4. Joseph had to forgive what others had done to him, while Paul had to forgive himself for what he had done to others. Which of these situations have you experienced the most, and which is easier or more difficult for you to face? If one of these situations is easier for you, why do you think that is?

5. Review Isaiah 54:17. Has there ever been a time when this passage has been particularly meaningful to you? What does this verse mean to you, and how has it helped you?

6. Think back through the teaching in this chapter regarding *lift* in the life of Joseph. List one thing you learned and one thing you can do right now that will allow you to begin accessing more of God's resurrection power—his *lift*—in your life.

CHAPTER SIX

Doing a Great Work: *Lift* in the Life of Nehemiah

"We are all faced with a series of great opportunities brilliantly disguised as impossible situations."
—Charles Swindoll

There is a tendency to want to start on top of the mountain. Who would not want to have pre-packaged success handed to him on a silver platter? Realistically, though, we often start with problems and have the responsibility of finding a way to bring "lift" to the situation—how to make it better and bring it into conformity to the will and pleasure of God. In the process of bringing lift to what may seem to be an impossible situation, *we* are lifted as well. Too often, people want to run away from problems instead of bringing solutions to the problems. But God has not called us to run away from problems; he has called us to be problem-solvers. Jesus came into a problem-filled world. Paul ministered to problem-filled churches. We live on a problem-filled planet.

Do not be disillusioned when you realize that your life is not exactly heaven on earth or some kind of utopia. Let God lift you, and determine to be a channel of his lifting power toward others. Instead of seeking to isolate ourselves from everything negative or unpleasant, we can seek to be an agent of God's resurrecting power for those in need of divine help.

Missionary C. T. Studd once remarked, "Some want to live within the sound of church or chapel bell; I want to run a rescue shop, within a yard of hell." This sentiment echoes Proverbs 24:11, which reads, "Deliver those who are drawn toward death, and hold back those stumbling to the slaughter." One of the best ways to experience lift in life is to make sure that you are committed to something bigger than yourself. God's big plan for all of us is that we minister the saving power of the gospel to others. God wants to lift everyone, and when we partner with him and reach out to lift others, we place ourselves in a position to be lifted as well. The Bible tells us that when we "water" others, we will be watered as well (Prov. 11:25). When we help people who can't pay us back, God sees to it that we are rewarded (Luke 14:14).

We have seen in previous chapters how lift worked in the lives of Paul and Joseph. In this chapter, we are going to examine lift in the life of Nehemiah. This great Old Testament figure held a highly respectable position in the administration of the Persian King Artaxerxes, but God had a greater assignment for him.

Many years after the destruction of Jerusalem, Nehemiah encountered some individuals who had recently visited the city as it was being resettled.

NEHEMIAH 1:2-4 (*NLT*)
2 I asked them about the Jews who had returned there from captivity and about how things were going in Jerusalem.

3 They said to me, "Things are not going well for those who returned to the province of Judah. They are in great trouble and disgrace. The wall of Jerusalem has been torn down, and the gates have been destroyed by fire."

4 When I heard this, I sat down and wept. In fact, for days I mourned, fasted, and prayed to the God of heaven.

Nehemiah did not have to care about the well-being of those in Jerusalem. He had a lucrative position in the king's palace in Persia. If he simply wanted to live for his own comfort and convenience, he could have tuned everyone else out and just enjoyed the security of his position. Rebuilding the broken walls was not just a good idea to Nehemiah; it was *God's* idea! The yearning, burning desire for the reconstruction of those walls became part of the very fabric of Nehemiah's being.

One of the great lessons from Nehemiah is this: If you are going to significantly lift others, it will probably be in spite of tremendous opposition. Nehemiah had to overcome challenges and resistance from without and from within. Consider some of the problems he encountered:

- The project itself—the residents were in great distress and reproach, the walls were broken down and the gates had been burnt (1:3). The city was in ruins (2:3).
- Nehemiah's enemies "scoffed contemptuously" at him and accused him of rebellion (2:19, *NLT*).
- Nehemiah and the Israelites were mocked, ridiculed, and insulted (4:1-3).
- Nehemiah's work force were threatened with military action (4:7-8).
- The people became weary, and it was difficult working amongst the rubbish (4:10).

- Some of the wealthier Israelites were taking advantage of those of lesser means and were exploiting them, charging them excessive interest on loans during a time of crisis (5:3-5)

After resisting the external challenges and working through the internal challenges, another potential pitfall appears. Nehemiah responds by magnifying the significance of his work:

NEHEMIAH 6:1-4

1 Now it happened when Sanballat, Tobiah, Geshem the Arab, and the rest of our enemies heard that I had rebuilt the wall, and that there were no breaks left in it (though at that time I had not hung the doors in the gates),

2 that Sanballat and Geshem sent to me, saying, "Come, let us meet together among the villages in the plain of Ono." But they thought to do me harm.

3 So I sent messengers to them, saying, "I am doing a great work, so that I cannot come down. Why should the work cease while I leave it and go down to you?"

4 But they sent me this message four times, and I answered them in the same manner.

Because of the diligence of Nehemiah and his fellow Israelites, great lift was taking place—the city walls were being wonderfully rebuilt! They had overcome several external challenges, but this final diversion had to be overcome as well.

This final challenged involved the issue of focus. Nehemiah had to stay focused on the task at hand. The enemy threw distraction and diversion at him, but Nehemiah resisted masterfully. How did Nehemiah do it? Consumed with his assignment from God, he states, "I am doing a great work, so that I cannot come down. Why should the work cease while I leave it and go down to you?" (6:3). This kind of resolve reminds me of an African proverb that states, "The lion does not turn around when a small dog barks." Nehemiah knew his objective and knew his priorities. He did not allow himself to be sidetracked by trying to please people who did not have his best interests at heart and did not respect the assignment God had given him. Other people may have seen a devastated city and a lot of rubbish, but Nehemiah saw the hand of God and a divine purpose. I don't know if the harm intended by Nehemiah's enemies was going to be physical in nature, or if they were going to try to get him to compromise in some way, but Nehemiah did not fall for the trap. The kind of focus exhibited by Nehemiah is the same kind of focus described by the great evangelist D. L. Moody:

> "The trouble with a great many men is that they spread themselves out over too much ground. They fail in everything. If they would only put their life into one channel, and keep it in, they would accomplish something. They make no impression, because they do a little work here and a little work there. . . . Lay yourselves on the altar of God, and then concentrate on some one work."[25]

Because Nehemiah focused on *one* thing, the wall was lifted—and because the wall was lifted, the city was lifted.

But What I'm Doing Doesn't Seem Very Great

We can get into trouble when we compare ourselves to some of the great heroes of the Bible. After all, most believers today do not restore

---

[25] Steve Miller, *D. L. Moody On Spiritual Leadership* (Chicago: Moody Publishers, 2004), 179.

safety and dignity to an entire city as Nehemiah did, nor do they become the prime minister of an empire and save God's chosen people from starvation as Joseph did. But it's important for us to realize that the greatness of what we do is not defined by the apparent grandeur or the overwhelming magnitude of our accomplishments. God himself is the one who defines what is great and what is not. While Scripture certainly teaches against a person arrogantly proclaiming one's own greatness, the Bible does not teach against genuine greatness. The Bible advocates true greatness, and Jesus even tells us how to achieve it. He states, "Whoever desires to become great among you, let him be your servant. And whoever desires to be first among you, let him be your slave" (Matt. 20:26-27). Servanthood is the pathway and key to greatness. Nehemiah was doing a great work because he was serving the plan and purpose of God—and because he was serving the *people* of God.

As God-followers, we must not be afraid of greatness. God is great, and he bestows greatness on his people for his own glory. Humility is always in order, but God-given greatness must be embraced and used for his purposes. Notice what God said to Abraham:

GENESIS 12:2
2 I will make you a great nation;
I will bless you and make your name great;
and you shall be a blessing.

GENESIS 15:1
1 Do not be afraid, Abram. I am your shield, your exceedingly great reward.

God does great things, and if we are going to interact with him, serve him, and represent him, we cannot get away from the idea of greatness. Remember that God sees and defines greatness through the lens and filter of servanthood. That is why Jesus states, "Whoever gives one of these little ones only a cup of cold water in the name of a disciple, assuredly, I say to you, he shall by no means lose his reward" (Matt. 10:42). When we do things in God's great name and for his great glory, he calls it great!

David "served his own generation by the will of God" (Acts 13:36). He experienced God's hand upon him in many ways, enabling him to accomplish various exploits for God's glory. In reflecting upon what God had helped him do, David reflects, "Your gentleness has made me great" (Psalm 18:35). The word "great" here literally means *increased.* The footnote of one Bible reads, "With thy meekness thou hast multiplied me." The *New International Version* reads, "You stoop down to make me great." In other words, David was saying, "God, your gentleness, your kindness, your mercy, and your stooping down to me have made me great—multiplying and increasing me!" The One who has always lifted people lifted David, enabling him to be great for God and do great things for God. This same One will *lift* and enable you.

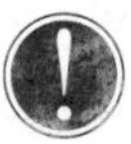 A Resurrection Declaration

Lord, I will not run away from the problems you have assigned me to solve. Rather, I choose to be a person who brings your solutions and your answers into these situations. Help me be an agent of your lifting and resurrecting power in situations that need your touch. Help me be willing to step out of my comfort zone and to step into challenging situations that require your wisdom and involvement. Help me be wise, resolute, and focused in bringing restoration to people and situations where you want to make a difference. By your power, I will not be disheartened by criticisms or thrown off track by distractions. May I be mindful of the value of every assignment you give me, and may I not pass up opportunities to be a blessing and help to others. Some people may not see my efforts as important, but I know that you consider every act of servanthood to be an act of greatness. In Jesus' name, I pray—amen.

Bonus Quotes

"You can often measure a person by the size of his dream."

—Robert H. Schuller

"The Holy Spirit cannot conquer the world with unbelief, nor can He save the world with a worldly Church. He calls for a crusade, a campaign, and an adventure of saving passion. For this enterprise He wants a separated, sanctified and sacrificial people."

—Samuel Chadwick

"It's no compliment to be a called a problem spotter, but the world loves problem solvers."

—Mark Sanborn

"You must keep your mind on the objective, not the obstacle."

—William Randolph Hearst

"Greatness lies, not in being strong, but in the right using of strength."

—Henry Ward Beecher

 Lyrics that Lift: Hymns of the Resurrection

From "Lift Up, Lift Up Your Voices Now" by John M. Neale (1851)

Lift up, lift up your voices now!
The whole wide world rejoices now;
The Lord has triumphed gloriously,
The Lord shall reign victoriously.

And all He did, and all He bare,
He gives us as our own to share;
And hope, and joy and peace begin,
For Christ has won, and man shall win.

O Victor, aid us in the fight,
And lead through death to realms of light;
We safely pass where Thou hast trod;
In Thee we die to rise to God.

Questions for Reflection and Discussion

1. Nehemiah's assignment took him from the comforts of the king's palace and put him in the middle of what appeared to be a big mess. Instead of getting to simply enjoy the perks of royalty, Nehemiah got to be a problem-solver. Can you relate to this kind of assignment? How?

2. When facing a potential distraction, Nehemiah's response was, "I am doing a great work, so that I cannot come down. Why should the work cease while I leave it and go down to you?" (Neh. 6:3). Is it possible to believe and say this about your own work without being arrogant? Why should you believe that you are doing great works, even if they are not highly esteemed by others?

3. Consider the African proverb "The lion does not turn around when a small dog barks." How does this maxim apply to Nehemiah, and how can it apply to you? What are some of the "barks" in your life that you need to ignore?

4. Review the quote by D. L. Moody on page 87. Most people have to handle numerous responsibilities in life. How can you realistically move toward the kind of focus and concentration that Moody describes?

5. How did Jesus define greatness, and why should believers not be afraid of greatness? How did David say he achieved greatness?

6. Think back through the teaching in this chapter regarding lift in the life of Nehemiah. List one thing you learned and one thing you can do right now that will allow you to begin accessing more of God's resurrection power—his *lift*—in your life.

CHAPTER SEVEN

'Blowing the Lid Off': *Lift* in the Life of Gideon

"The people who sat in darkness have seen a great light. And for those who lived in the land where death casts its shadow, a light has shined."

—Matthew 4:16

One of the recurring themes in Scripture is that of oppression followed by liberation. Some Christians today may not think of themselves as having ever been oppressed, but every believer recognizes that God set them free from the law of sin and death (Rom. 8:1). In the Old Testament, God told his people to share with the next generation how God had liberated them.

DEUTERONOMY 6:21-23

21 Then you shall say to your son: "We were slaves of Pharaoh in Egypt, and the Lord brought us out of Egypt with a mighty hand;

22 and the Lord showed signs and wonders before our eyes, great and severe, against Egypt, Pharaoh, and all his household.

23 Then He brought us out from there, that He might bring us in, to give us the land of which He swore to our fathers.

If you fail to recognize the depths (or the potential depths) from which God delivered you, you will probably not appreciate where you are or value the place where you are headed.

In the gospels, Luke describes an immoral woman who showed great honor toward Jesus and relates Jesus' statement concerning her: "Her sins—and they are many—have been forgiven, so she has shown me much love. But a person who is forgiven little shows only little love" (Luke 7:47, *NLT*). You may never have committed adultery, but Jesus teaches that "whoever looks at a woman to lust for her has already committed adultery with her in his heart" (Matt. 5:28). Scripture teaches that everyone needs forgiveness! When God "blows the lid off" of all that has oppressed us, we can ascend into freedom and liberty with heartfelt gratitude and appreciation.

While God delights in setting people free, there is an enemy determined to keep people in bondage. The story of Gideon in the Old Testament provides an example of how God liberates his people from oppression. The Midianites and other groups had been raiding Israel during harvest seasons, taking their crops and livestock by force. These raids were so severe that Scripture says, "Israel was reduced to starvation by the Midianites" (Judg. 6:6, *NLT*). Now *that* is oppression! But God raised up a deliverer—an unlikely deliverer—named Gideon.

Like the rest of the Israelites, Gideon was fearful and intimidated by the hostile marauding forces, but God saw potential and possibilities in Gideon that Gideon did not see in himself. When the angel of the Lord appeared, he not only told Gideon of his assignment to deliver the Israelites from the oppression of the Midianites, but he also greeted Gideon with a most surprising salutation. The angel said, "Mighty hero, the Lord is with you!" (Judg. 6:12, *NLT*). After some negative complaining, Gideon then asked, "How can I rescue Israel? My clan is the weakest in the whole tribe of Manasseh, and I am the least in my entire family!" (Judg. 6:15, *NLT*).

Every person God raises up still has to rely on God's strength to accomplish the divine assignment. Likewise, it was made clear to Gideon that he didn't have to carry out his assignment in his own strength; God's power and ability would be at work in and through him (Judg. 6:14,16). For Gideon to step into his God-ordained role, he had to overcome his negativity, insecurity, and sense of inferiority—this "lid" that kept him trapped, or held back, had to be blasted off by the power of God.

There are lies that the enemy commonly feeds into the minds of people to try to keep them from rising to their potential and fulfilling their destiny. Here are three lies that were used on Gideon and may have been used on you at some point: 1) You have little value—you are worthless; 2) you have little faith—you are faithless; and 3) you have little ability—you are helpless. Let's look at each of these lies individually, and see how God empowers us to respond to each of them.

Lie #1: You have little value—you are worthless.

One of the things that keeps people oppressed is the false belief that they have little or no value. Many have been demeaned, degraded, and devalued by the words and actions of others. They have been made to feel marginalized through the rejection, abuse, and dismissiveness of others. They feel that they have been used and then discarded when they were of no more use. One of the great skills a person can develop in life is the ability to refuse others' projections of value or worth. In other words, I have to be able to say, "My value as a human being is not determined by your opinions, words, or actions toward me. Other people may devalue me, but God determines my real value, and he says I am valuable. I am who God says I am."

If you are going to determine the value of a physical object, one of the things to consider is what someone is willing to pay for it. No one is willing to pay $5,000 for a common pencil because a pencil is not worth that much. Peter teaches that the ransom God paid for us was "the precious blood of Christ, the sinless, spotless Lamb of God" (1 Pet. 1:18-19, *NLT*). The price paid for us tells us what we are worth to God. How could you place a value on the very blood of Christ? It is of inestimable worth. Follow the reasoning: God must see us as very valuable and precious if he was willing to purchase us with the blood of his Son.

Consider some of the following facts that speak to our value in God's eyes:

- God has loved us with an everlasting love. He never started loving us (because he has loved us from eternity past), and he will never stop loving us. Jeremiah 31:3 says, "I have loved you with an everlasting love; therefore with lovingkindness I have drawn you."
- We did not choose him; he chose us (John 15:16).
- We did not pursue God; he pursued us. Jesus says, "The Son of Man has come to seek and to save that which was lost" (Luke 19:10).
- We did not die for him; he died for us. Paul teaches, "God demonstrates His own love toward us, in that while we were still sinners, Christ died for us" (Rom. 5:8).
- When we surrendered our lives to Jesus' lordship, there was a celebration in heaven (Luke 15:7). God doesn't merely tolerate us; he celebrates us as his beloved children.

- God loved us before we ever thought of loving him. The Apostle John writes, "This is real love—not that we loved God, but that he loved us and sent his Son as a sacrifice to take away our sins" (1 John 4:10, *NLT*).

We are not afterthoughts in the plan of God. We are not accidents that he is trying to do something with. God loved us before the foundation of the world; furthermore, he knew us and established a wonderful plan for our lives before we were even born. We are the object and recipient of eternal love!

It is also important to recognize that God's love for us is not restricted to the act of Jesus dying on the cross. Romans 8:32 in *The Message* states, "If God didn't hesitate to put everything on the line for us, embracing our condition and exposing himself to the worst by sending his own Son, is there anything else he wouldn't gladly and freely do for us?" Do not let the devil tell you that you have no value! Do not let yourself suffer under the bondage of guilt, shame, condemnation, and inferiority when God has already set you free! God has no second-class children; you are royalty—you belong to the Most High God. When the devil tells you that you have little value, that you are worthless, respond back to him: "I am of great value. I have been purchased with the blood of Jesus. And I am worthy, because God has made me worthy."

Lie #2: You have little faith—you are faithless.

Many Christians struggle at times with feeling as if they do not have enough faith. When this happens, they can wrestle with guilt and inferiority, even to the point of believing that God is overwhelmingly disappointed with them. Some get in a vicious cycle of trying to have more faith, and as long as the focus is on one's own faith (or lack thereof), the frustration will continue. The key to having strong faith is not to focus on faith, but to focus on the very object of faith—God himself. When we focus on the greatness of God and feed upon his Word, our faith will grow.

Other ministers have noted and remarked on this important principle. Consider the following observations:

- In a letter to famed missionary J. Hudson Taylor, John McCarthy wrote, "But how to get faith strengthened? Not by striving after faith, but by resting on the Faithful One."
- Charles Spurgeon noted, "The Puritans were accustomed to explain faith by the word 'recumbency.' It meant leaning upon a thing. Lean with all your weight upon Christ. It would be a better illustration still if I said, fall at full length, and lie on the Rock of Ages."
- Vance Havner said, "Faith has no value of its own, it has value only as it connects us with Him. It is a trick of Satan to get us occupied with examining our faith instead of resting in the Faithful One."
- Stuart Briscoe remarked, "Faith is only as valid as its object. You could have tremendous faith in very thin ice and drown. . . . You could have very little faith in very thick ice and be perfectly secure."

Here are some additional thoughts to help us keep faith in perspective.

Faith is a gift from God. It is not something we generate within ourselves.

We see this in Ephesians 2:8: "For by grace you have been saved through faith, and that not of yourselves; it is the gift of God."

Faith is a divine result proceeding from a divine influence.

Romans 10:17 says, "So then faith comes by hearing, and hearing by the word of God."

Our faith can grow as we come to know and trust God more.

Paul told one group of believers, "Your faith grows exceedingly" (2 Thess. 1:3). The Bible refers to "little faith" (Matt. 6:30), "weak faith" (Rom. 14:1), "great faith" (Matt. 8:10), being "full of faith" (Acts 6:5), and being "strengthened in faith" (Acts 16:5).

We don't have to wait until we have great faith before we begin trusting God.

Jesus challenged a man who needed help by telling him, "If you can believe, all things are possible to him who believes." The man honestly responded, "Lord, I believe; help my unbelief!" (Mark 9:23-24). I find it encouraging that Jesus did not rebuke this man and send him away, saying, "That is unacceptable! Do not come back here until your faith is perfect." While we love the idea of aspiring to great faith, in this case, Jesus met the man where he was.

Similarly, while Jesus acknowledged and encouraged great faith, he did not present the idea that a person had to achieve some super-level of spirituality before he could see God do great things. Jesus teaches his disciples, "If you had faith even as small as a mustard seed, you could say to this mountain, 'Move from here to there,' and it would move. Nothing would be impossible'" (Matt. 17:20, *NLT*). The key to a small seed producing results is that it *be planted*. Likewise, the key to even small bit of faith producing results is that it *be used*—that it be *acted upon*. Gideon began acting on what God showed him even when he felt inferior, and the results followed.

When you are tempted to focus on yourself and your seemingly small faith, put your eyes on God and his Word, the source of faith. Declare,

"God, you have given me grace and faith—they are gifts from you to me. I accept them. Faith comes to me through your Word and your precious promises to me. My faith is based on who you are—on your character and on your nature. My faith is in a great God, and as I keep my eyes on you, I believe my faith and trust in you will continue to grow."

Lie #3: You have little ability—you are purposeless.

Jesus did an amazing thing when he came to this earth: "He set aside the privileges of deity and took on the status of a slave, became human" (Phil. 2:7, *MSG*). As a result, Jesus relied entirely upon the empowerment of his Father and the anointing of the Holy Spirit to do all that he did. This is why Jesus states, "I can of myself do nothing" (John 5:30) and, "the Father who dwells in me does the works" (John 14:10). Gideon's problem is that he focused on himself—his own inadequacies and shortcomings. Jesus, however, focused on the ability, nature, and goodness of God. It would benefit all of us if we focused more on God and less on ourselves. When we establish the right mindset, we will say with Paul, "I can do all things through Christ who strengthens me" (Phil. 4:13).

If a Christian believes he has little or no value and little or no faith, it is very likely that he will also feel that he has no purpose and little to offer others. Sometimes this feeling is exacerbated when he looks around and sees others who have tremendous gifts and extraordinary talents. The comparison trap has snagged many believers and rendered them inactive because they don't feel that they can preach or sing or pray like someone else. Because they are so busy being intimidated by someone else's talents, they may never discover their own. It is good to keep in mind that while there are a few people here and there with exceptional gifts, most of us have what may seem to be ordinary, less exciting gifts. But this does not mean that we cannot be a great help and blessing to others through our Spirit-infused efforts and love-based labors.

Likewise, some pastors feel insecure because they don't have a mega-church, but the important thing is that each of us is faithful serving God in the role that he has given us. Gideon felt like God could not use him because he was the least in his entire family, but God had other plans. This reminds me a bit of what God spoke to Israel through Moses:

DEUTERONOMY 7:7-8 (*NLT*)
7 "The Lord did not set his heart on you and choose you because you were more numerous than other nations, for you were the smallest of all nations!

8 Rather, it was simply that the Lord loves you, and he was keeping the oath he had sworn to your ancestors. That is why the Lord rescued you with such a strong hand from your slavery and from the oppressive hand of Pharaoh, king of Egypt.

There is nothing wrong with starting small, and there is nothing wrong with doing what some may consider small endeavors. You may think that what you are doing is small and unimportant, but God assesses things differently than humans do. If you are walking in love and demonstrating the fruit of the spirit in your life—being an example of Christlikeness to others, being salt and light—then you are doing something very important.

If you are a highly gifted and doing awesome things, then you might already think you are fulfilling a great purpose. But if you are like the majority of us, then it may help you to be reminded that God seems to delight in taking things that seem small and insignificant from a human perspective and turning them into powerful blessings! Consider these biblical examples:

- Moses had a rod, and the greatest empire in the world was brought to its knees.
- Rahab had a scarlet thread, and her whole household was saved.
- Samson had a donkey's jawbone, and God enabled him to slay a thousand men.
- David had a sling, and the giant was defeated.
- The widow woman had a pot of oil, and great provision came.
- The little boy had a few loaves and fishes, and Jesus fed a multitude.
- Dorcas had a needle and thread, and many were blessed.

The issue is not how famous you are or whether others are impressed by you. What really matters can summed up in two questions: "What do you have?" and "What are you doing with it?"

Paul wanted to make sure that the Roman believers did not corrupt their sense of usefulness and purposefulness by comparing themselves with others. He advised them that we do not all have "the same function;" rather, we all have "gifts differing according to the grace that is given to us" (Rom. 12:4, 6). We each have purpose, responsibilities, and assignments to fulfill, and that is where we will find our greatest personal fulfillment *and* provide our greatest benefit to others.

While Gideon originally suffered from a low opinion of himself, he turned his attention to what God said about him and God "blew the lid off" of his insecurities and sense of inferiority. He went on to do great things for God and God's people. We, too, can also rise above self-imposed limitations and serve God's purpose in our generation. To do this, we need to remember these three powerful truths: 1) We have great value and worth before God; 2) we have faith—we can respond to and act on God's Word, and 3) we have gifts from God—when we use them in serving others, we find purpose and fulfillment. When we live in accordance to these three powerful truths, God lifts us from where we are to where he wants us to be.

❗ A Resurrection Declaration

Lord, thank you that you are a liberator and that it is your nature to set people free, including me. You never want me to forget how good you have been to me or forget the many things from which you have rescued me. Thank you that you have allowed me to partner with you in demonstrating your liberating nature to others, and thank you for the assignments you have given me and the ones yet to come. Help me not to feel overwhelmed, inferior, intimidated, or incompetent concerning any task you give me. I know that your power and your ability are what really matters. Whatever you call me to do, you will empower me to accomplish it. Because of Jesus, I believe that I have great value in your eyes; I believe that you have given me faith through your Word; and I believe that you give me ability through the Holy Spirit. Lord, you can take gifts and assignments that the world might consider insignificant and generate great blessings through them, so thank you for helping me to be faithful with all that you enable me to do. In Jesus' name, I pray—amen.

Bonus Quotes

"We are adopted into God's family through the resurrection of Christ from the dead in which he paid all our obligations to sin, the law, and the devil, in whose family we once lived. Our old status lies in his tomb. A new status is ours through his resurrection."

—Sinclair B. Ferguson

"Imagine what your life will look like when you have broken the bondage of fear."

—Bruce Wilkinson

"Many Christians estimate difficulty in the light of their own resources, and thus they attempt very little and they always fail. All giants have been weak men who did great things for God because they reckoned on His power and presence to be with them."

—Hudson Taylor

"God uses ordinary people who are obedient to Him to do extraordinary things."

—John Maxwell

"It is impossible for that man to despair who remembers that his Helper is omnipotent."

—Jeremy Taylor

Lyrics that Lift: Hymns of the Resurrection

From "The Day of Resurrection" by John of Damascus (8th Century)

The day of resurrection!
Earth, tell it out abroad;
The passover of gladness,
The passover of God.

From death to life eternal,
From earth unto the sky,
Our Christ hath brought us over,
With hymns of victory.

Now let the heavens be joyful!
Let earth the song begin!
Let the round world keep triumph,
And all that is therein!

Let all things seen and unseen
Their notes in gladness blend,
For Christ the Lord hath risen,
Our joy that hath no end.

 Questions for Reflection and Discussion

1. Why did Gideon feel like he was unlikely to be chosen by God? What personal issues did Gideon have to overcome in order to accept God's call? Can you relate to any of the feelings Gideon expressed?
2. Has there ever been a time when you did not see yourself as having value? How did that self-perception affect you? How do you see yourself today in terms of value and worth? Upon what do you base your assessment?
3. Have you ever struggled with thinking that you did not have enough faith? What did you do (or how did God help you) to address this issue? What are your thoughts about not trying to have a great *faith* but recognizing that your faith is in a great *God*?
4. Have you ever fallen into the comparison trap? When you compared yourself and your abilities to those of someone else, what effect did it have on you? What have you done to overcome this trap?
5. We read in this chapter that God seems to take delight in using small things for his glory (e.g., Moses' rod, David's sling, the little boy's lunch, and so forth). Is there something in your life that seems like a small talent, skill, or opportunity that you have seen God turn into a blessing for others? Is there something in your life that you have withheld from using to serve others because you have not esteemed it highly enough?
6. Think back through the teaching in this chapter regarding lift in the life of Gideon. List one thing you learned and one thing you can do right now that will allow you to begin accessing more of God's resurrection power—his *lift*—in your life.

SECTION III

Experiencing *Lift* in Our Lives

CHAPTER EIGHT

The Higher Law Leads to the Higher Life

Then will you delight yourself in the Lord, and I will make you to ride on the high places of the earth.

—Isaiah 58:14

When God created the universe, he established laws, or principles, by which things function and operate. For example, in the first chapter of Genesis, there are several references to the fact that botanical and biological life would reproduce after its own kind. The intricate order and organization in this universe suggests the existence and involvement of an amazingly brilliant, wise, and powerful God. There are natural laws such as those that pertain to thermodynamics, motion, and gravity, and there are spiritual laws that we find described in Scripture.

One of the first principles that God communicated to man is described on the first pages of the Bible:

GENESIS 2:16-17

16 And the Lord commanded the man, saying, "Of every tree of the garden you may freely eat;

17 but of the tree of the knowledge of good and evil you shall not eat, for in the day that you eat of it you shall surely die."

Here we see the principle of free will—man could choose to obey God or not—but the consequences of man's choice were established by a law. *Life* was the initial status quo, but *death*, another word for "separation," was the inevitable consequence that would follow disobedience. This notion of obey=life/disobey=death recurs multiple times throughout Scripture. This is evidence of the fact that God has established laws that govern our existence.

A clear example of such laws is when God tells Israel through Moses, "I have set before you life and death, blessing and cursing; therefore choose life, that both you and your descendants may live" (Deut. 30:19). A nearly identical articulation is expressed through Jeremiah: "Thus says the Lord: 'Behold, I set before you the way of life and the way of death'" (Jer. 21:8). I do not want to depersonalize this issue because God is a personal being, but he has established laws—both naturally and spiritually—that affect every human being. In order to experience the kind of life God intends, it behooves us to learn the principles he has established and to walk in his ways.

While God reveals his principles throughout the Bible, there is a very high concentration of them in the Book of Proverbs. This wonderful collection of writings does not simply present principles of God's wisdom and the benefits of choosing wisdom, but it also reveals the pain that choosing foolishness will bring into the lives of those who walk that path. Some paths lead to life; others lead to death. It is correct to say that acting upon the higher laws leads to a higher life—a higher quality of life. Similarly, following lower laws leads to a lower quality of life.

It is important that we do not perceive these laws to be the law of sin and death (from which we've been redeemed) or the old Jewish law (that some Pharisees turned into legalism). Rather, we should simply understand that God has invested his life and his power in his Word, and in that Word are principles for us to live by. It makes sense, then, to say that living by these principles—or, living according to God's Word—will in turn make us recipients of God's power and life.

Remember, Jesus said, "I am the resurrection and the life" (John 11:25). Note that life and resurrection are connected. It makes perfect sense that a person who identifies himself as "the resurrection" would lift his followers into a higher life! Consider these other truths:

- Jesus is called "the Word of life" (1 John 1:1).
- Jesus states, "The words that I speak to you are spirit, and they are life" (John 6:63).
- *The Message* renders John 6:63, "Every word I've spoken to you is a Spirit-word, and so it is life-making."
- Paul calls the message of the New Testament "the word of life" (Phil. 2:6).

There is a definite relationship between God's Word and God's kind of life—both the creative, sustaining power that God used (and uses) to give life to the world and the resurrection power that God uses to give life to the dead. We cannot have one without the other.

Hebrews 11:3 teaches that "the worlds were framed by the word of God," and Hebrews 1:3 tells us that God "sustains all things by his powerful word" (*NET*). Consider Proverbs 4:20-22, which says, "My child, pay attention to what I say. Listen carefully to *my words*. Don't lose sight of them. Let them penetrate deep into your heart, for they *bring life to those who find them, and healing to their whole body*" (*NLT*, emphasis mine).

I realize that the word "resurrection" is not used in this passage, but isn't *life* the very essence of what resurrection is all about—God's life being released in our life, changing us, and lifting us to a higher level?

Whatever God's Word communicates and instructs us to do is going to be the higher principle (or law) that leads us to a higher life. Another example of there being a choice between higher and lower, life and death, good and evil is observable in this admonition from Peter:

> **1 PETER 4:10-12 (*NLT*)**
> **10 For the Scriptures say, "If you want to enjoy life and see many happy days, keep your tongue from speaking evil and your lips from telling lies.**
>
> **11 Turn away from evil and do good. Search for peace, and work to maintain it.**
>
> **12 The eyes of the Lord watch over those who do right, and his ears are open to their prayers. But the Lord turns his face against those who do evil."**

Notice that there are both positive and negative elements to Peter's instructions. There are negative elements to avoid and positive aspects to embrace. If we do as Scripture says, we experience a lift—the higher law will lead us to a higher life. If we habitually disobey the Bible, we will experience a lower quality of existence—the lower law will lead us to a lower life.

Before any of us were born again, there was a law at work against us—we were "dead in trespasses and sins" (Eph. 2:1). This law had a strong downward pull on us. The sin principle that is at work in the world degrades and defiles those under its influence. Paul proceeds to say that we were governed by "the spirit who now works in the sons of disobedience, among whom also we all once conducted ourselves in the lusts of our flesh, fulfilling the desires of the flesh and of the mind, and were by nature children of wrath, just as the others" (Eph. 2:3). That was the lower law, and the more it influenced us, the more it dragged us down. However, God provided a higher law that would not only pull us out of the death spiral but would also give us life and set us on an upward trajectory.

> **EPHESIANS 2:4-6**
> **4 But God, who is rich in mercy, because of his great love with which he loved us,**
>
> **5 even when we were dead in trespasses, made us alive together with Christ (by grace you have been saved),**
>
> **6 and raised us up together, and made us sit together in the heavenly places in Christ Jesus.**

The lower law dominated us until the higher law set us free! The higher law leads us to a higher life!

The little conjunction in Ephesians 2:4—the word "but"—makes all the difference in the world. It means that there is something (or Someone) on the other side of the problem. We were dead—*but God.* His intervention does more than give us a new beginning and a new opportunity; it brings the higher law of his grace flooding into our lives—lifting us and changing everything.

Let's look at some other scriptures that demonstrate the higher law leads us to the higher life. I have emphasized the word "but" in each of these verses to bring your attention to the kind of "before and after" difference God makes in the lives of his people:

- "David was greatly distressed, for the people spoke of stoning him, because the soul of all the people was grieved, every man for his sons and his daughters. *But* David strengthened himself in the Lord his God" (1 Sam. 30:6).

- "In the world you will have tribulation; *but* be of good cheer, I have overcome the world" (John 16:33).
- "The wages of sin is death, *but* the gift of God is eternal life in Christ Jesus our Lord" (Rom. 6:23).
- "Let us walk properly, as in the day, not in revelry and drunkenness, not in lewdness and lust, not in strife and envy. *But* put on the Lord Jesus Christ, and make no provision for the flesh, to fulfill its lusts" (Rom. 13:13-14).
- "He who sows to his flesh will of the flesh reap corruption, *but* he who sows to the Spirit will of the Spirit reap everlasting life" (Gal. 6:8).
- "No temptation has overtaken you except such as is common to man; *but* God is faithful, who will not allow you to be tempted beyond what you are able, *but* with the temptation will also make the way of escape, that you may be able to bear it" (1 Cor. 10:13).
- "I am the least of the apostles, who am not worthy to be called an apostle, because I persecuted the church of God. *But* by the grace of God I am what I am" (1 Cor. 15:9-10).

I particularly like Paul's statement in this last passage because there is a reference to the historical facts of Paul's life *and* a reference to the grace of God—a redemptive and eternal reality. The eternal reality of God's grace triumphs over the historical fact of Paul's previous sin. Because all of us have sinned, every one of us has historical facts that work against us, but because of grace—what God has done for us through Jesus—there is an eternal reality that overrides, supersedes, and transcends the historical facts. We, then, become the recipients of God's goodness, not the victims of our own past. When we accept God's provision of redemption, we can be tremendously thankful as we read Paul's declaration: "The power of the life-giving Spirit has freed you from the power of sin that leads to death" (Rom. 8:2, *NLT*).

The prophet Isaiah powerfully articulates the difference between the level that God operates on (and invites us up to) and the level where people normally live. It is important to note that God not only points out the difference between where he is and where we are, but he also communicates how we can begin to live at a higher level—at the level where he is.

ISAIAH 55:8-11 (*NLT*)
8 "My thoughts are nothing like your thoughts," says the Lord. "And my ways are far beyond anything you could imagine.
9 For just as the heavens are higher than the earth, so my ways are higher than your ways and my thoughts higher than your thoughts.
10 The rain and snow come down from the heavens and stay on the ground to water the earth. They cause the grain to grow, producing seed for the farmer and bread for the hungry.
11 It is the same with my word. I send it out, and it always produces fruit. It will accomplish all I want it to, and it will prosper everywhere I send it."

Some who read this passage in Isaiah tend to focus only on the first part—that God's thoughts and ways are far above ours. But we need to read the second part as well: God has sent his Word, and the idea here, in full context, is that God's Word will enable us to think his thoughts and walk in his ways. God's Word will produce fruit in our lives when we receive it, apply it to our life, and live by it. God's Word, with all of its inherent life and power, will lift us up and enable us to walk in higher degrees of godliness, wisdom, and virtue.

The point that I want to make in this chapter is that the higher law leads to a higher life. This idea is not hyper-mystical or an excessively spiritual one. It has very practical ramifications. For example, consider a man who was raised in a dysfunctional home. Maybe his dad was merely distant and aloof; perhaps his dad was abusive or unfaithful, or struggled with substance abuse. As this man moves from childhood into adulthood, he realizes that his earthly father's example was not the best. He has a choice to make. If he is negatively influenced by his dad's example and chooses to follow in his father's footsteps, his own marriage and family will be negatively affected and pulled downward. But if he reads in God's Word how a man should treat his wife and children, commits himself to loving his wife as Christ loves the Church, and determines to raise his children in the nurture and admonition of the Lord, this man will be lifted to a higher life. He will walk in love and manifest the fruit of the spirit in his home. In short, he will have yielded to a higher law, and generally speaking, his family will be blessed because he took that route. The higher law leads to a higher life!

I am not saying that if you choose the higher laws—believing, speaking, and acting in line with God's Word—that you will never encounter situations in life that negatively impact you. What I am saying is that when you choose God's ways, you won't sabotage yourself and create the additional problems that come through disobedience and from cooperating with the law of sin and death that is operating in the world. It is certainly true that some people choose the higher law and then encounter opposition or even persecution. However, when you walk in the higher law, you have God's presence, wisdom, and ability working in your life to help you overcome whatever opposition comes against you.

We referenced Joseph in a previous chapter, and even though he was consistently battered after choosing the higher law, God ultimately brought him to the top. Today we see people who are corrupt and still seem to prosper. This kind of contradiction was the basis of King David's frustration in Psalm chapter 37 and 73. But David came to the realization that God's people must look at the long-term picture. The wicked may appear to prosper for a time, but they will ultimately fall. The righteous may seem to falter for a season, but ultimately (and eternally), they will experience blessing.

The prophet Habakkuk was frustrated because he was not seeing the results he wanted to see, but he finally expressed the insight that helped him greatly (and has since helped countless others):

> **HABAKKUK 3:17-19**
> **17 Though the fig tree may not blossom, nor fruit be on the vines; though the labor of the olive may fail, and the fields yield no food; though the flock may be cut off from the fold, and there be no herd in the stalls—**
>
> **18 Yet I will rejoice in the Lord, I will joy in the God of my salvation.**
>
> **19 The Lord God is my strength; he will make my feet like deer's feet, and he will make me walk on my high hills.**

Even the prophet Habakkuk recognized the concept of lift. Even though nothing seemed to be going right at the moment, Habakkuk was certain that God would eventually lift him up and enable him to walk in high places! Remember that the higher law leads to the higher life.

A Resurrection Declaration

Lord, thank you that you are a God of brilliant laws and amazing order. You have communicated the principles governing life in your Word, and the Holy Spirit teaches me concerning your ways. You asked me to choose, and I choose life and blessing. I choose the way of truth as revealed in your Word, and your Word brings life and healing to my whole body. Thank you that even though I was dead in trespasses and sin, your great mercy prevailed, and now I have been made alive together with Christ—raised with him and made to sit with him in heavenly places. The higher law has led me into a higher life. Your ways and thoughts are higher than mine, but thank you for sending your Word so that I can learn to think your thoughts and walk in your ways. Even when facing situations and circumstances that are difficult, I choose to trust in you and rejoice in you. I believe that you will help me to walk in high places. In Jesus' name, I pray—amen.

Bonus Quotes

"It is always more easy to discover and proclaim general principles than it is to apply them."

—Winston Churchill

"Wisdom consists of the anticipation of consequences."

—Norman Cousins

"There is a choice you have to make in everything you do. So keep in mind that in the end, the choice you make, makes you."

—John Wooden

"Every choice you make has an end result."

—Zig Ziglar

"If you do what you should not, you must bear what you would not."

—Benjamin Franklin

 Lyrics that Lift: Hymns of the Resurrection

From "All Hail, Thou Resurrection" by William H. Havergal (1867)

All hail, Thou resurrection!
All hail, Thou life and light!
All hail, Thou self perfection,
Sole source of grace and might!

Thy Church, O Christ, now greets Thee,
Uprising from the grave;
And every eye that meets Thee
Beholds Thee strong to save.

Questions for Reflection and Discussion

1. In this chapter, we saw that God set before his people life and death and asked them to choose. How do you, as a believer, choose life? How do you practically express your choice through your thoughts, beliefs, words, and actions?

2. Review First Peter 4:10-12. How can following such simple instructions be instrumental in determining the type of environment and kind of outcomes we experience in life?

3. We studied several scriptures in which an intervention of some kind took place. Someone was headed one direction, but God intervened. For example, Paul states, "I am the least of the apostles, who am not worthy to be called an apostle, because I persecuted the church of God. *But* by the grace of God I am what I am" (1 Cor. 15:9-10, emphasis mine). If you were to write a summary statement about your life, and insert God's intervention, how would that sentence read?

4. Review Isaiah 55:8-11. Was this passage written to demonstrate that we can never attain God's ways or comprehend his thoughts? Or was it written to show us *how* to attain to his ways and *how* to comprehend his thoughts? If it is the latter, explain what we must do to move towards this higher life.

5. Review Habakkuk 3:17-19. Is it possible to experience lift—to walk in high places with God—even when circumstances are not favorable? Have you ever faced a time in your life when circumstances were very challenging, and yet you sensed the grace of God giving you great *lift* on the inside?

6. Think back through the teaching in this chapter regarding how the higher law leads to a higher life. List one thing you learned and one thing you can do right now that will allow you to begin accessing more of God's resurrection power—his *lift*—in your life.

CHAPTER NINE

Seven 'Unders' That Will Put You Over

If you fully obey the Lord your God and carefully keep all his commands that I am giving you today, the Lord your God will set you high above all the nations of the world. If you listen to these commands of the Lord your God that I am giving you today, and if you carefully obey them, the Lord will make you the head and not the tail, and you will always be on top and never at the bottom.

Deuteronomy 28:1,13 (*NLT*)

People are continually looking for that special something that will give them an edge in life. They are looking for an advantage, something that will raise them to a higher level of living. People don't want to be *under* the weather, *under* pressure, or *under* the circumstances. People want to rise above the challenges and pressures of life and enjoy God's blessings and the victory he offers his children.

Some people think the way to "get to the top" is to scrap and scrape and claw. Some resort to breaking rules and even breaking the law, violating good ethics and trampling other people in their efforts to get ahead. It's true that people can get ahead in some things that way, but the damage to one's soul and one's conscience (not to mention the people they hurt) is such that they cannot truly enjoy what they have supposedly achieved. Built on such a sorry foundation, much of what they gain is often eventually lost. This is why Proverbs 10:22 states, "The blessing of the Lord makes one rich, and he adds no sorrow with it."

There is nothing wrong with wanting to excel, advance, and do well in life, but we ought to achieve success with a godly attitude and through godly means. Our work needs to be done for God's glory, not to feed carnal ambition. Jesus states, "If anyone serves me, him my Father will honor" (John 12:26). If God honors us, that is certainly a good thing. But Jesus also speaks of those "who receive honor from one another" and who "do not seek the honor that comes from the only God" (John 5:44). Clearly, there is a problem when we prefer the recognition and praise of people to that of pleasing God. Humbling ourselves to serve God for his pleasure will always bring better long-term results than proudly seeking the approval of men. Proverbs 29:23 echoes this truth, saying, "Pride ends in humiliation, while humility brings honor" (*NLT*).

Jesus taught the simple principle that "whoever exalts himself will be humbled, and he who humbles himself will be exalted" (Matt. 23:12). Jesus also gave us a vivid illustration of what happens to those who are properly exalted as opposed to those who exalt themselves.

LUKE 14:7-10 (*NLT*)

7 When Jesus noticed that all who had come to the dinner were trying to sit in the seats of honor near the head of the table, he gave them this advice:

8 "When you are invited to a wedding feast, don't sit in the seat of honor. What if someone who is more distinguished than you has also been invited?

9 The host will come and say, 'Give this person your seat.' Then you will be embarrassed, and you will have to take whatever seat is left at the foot of the table!

10 "Instead, take the lowest place at the foot of the table. Then when your host sees you, he will come and say, 'Friend, we have a better place for you!' Then you will be honored in front of all the other guests.

Clearly, God has a way of exalting people, and so does Satan. God sustains those he raises up, but when Satan exalts someone, that person will ultimately come crashing down. Paul describes the method of the antichrist when he writes, "He will exalt himself and defy everything that people call god and every object of worship. He will even sit in the temple of God, claiming that he himself is God" (2 Thess. 2:4, *NLT*). In Psalm chapter 37 and 73, King David expresses significant angst and consternation over seeing ungodly men prosper. However, as he processes his anger and frustration, he comes to the realization that he can trust God to take care of him, and that the end result of the ungodly—no matter how successful they look at that moment—is not to be envied.

I want to present seven principles from Scripture that all convey some concept related to the term "under." When diligently practiced, each of these principles will bring lift into a believer's life.

1. Stay *under* the mighty hand of God.

Peter presents a beautiful directive and subsequent promise, saying, "Humble yourselves therefore under the mighty hand of God, that he may exalt you in due time" (1 Pet. 5:6). In Scripture, "the hand of God" often refers to the fact that God is powerfully and yet tenderly holding his children. His "hand" refers to his care, attention, and protection over our lives. Note these examples from the Bible (emphasis is mine):

- "In your presence is fullness of joy; at your right *hand* are pleasures forevermore" (Psalm 16:11).
- "I will strengthen you and help you. I will hold you up with my victorious right *hand*" (Isa. 41:10).
- "I will not forget you. See, I have inscribed you on the palms of my *hands*" (Isa. 49:15-16).
- Daniel prayed to God, "[You] brought your people out of the land of Egypt with a mighty *hand*" (Dan. 9:15).
- Jesus teaches, "My Father has given them to me, and he is more powerful than anyone else. No one can snatch them from the Father's *hand*" (John 10:29, *NLT*).

Daniel experienced the exalting hand of God—a lift that came when he humbled himself under God's mighty hand. The Bible teaches that because of his reverential respect toward God, Daniel was made ten times better than his peers (Dan. 1:20).

Augustine comments, "There is something in humility which strangely exalts the heart." In one sense, Christianity is a paradox. We go up by going down. We go over by going under. The person who does not trust in God or acknowledge him may strive relentlessly to reach the pinnacle of success. However, without God's help, he will ultimately fall. The person who honors God and acknowledges him in all things will have God's help and blessing.

Always remember that God is interested in lifting you up. Maintain a humble attitude in all things. Be sure to give God credit and glory for all of the good that comes into your life. Even though your human efforts may have played a part in earning the success you receive, just remember whose air it was that you were breathing while you were working, and who gave you the strength, knowledge, and gifts to make your success possible! I wholeheartedly agree with Fred Smith's observation: "Humility is not denying the power you have. It is realizing that the power comes through you, not from you." Staying under the mighty hand of God will result in your being powerfully lifted up by God!

2. Stay *under* grace.

Grace is God's overwhelming love and kindness manifested toward us in the Person and work of Jesus and in the Holy Spirit. When we receive Jesus, trusting in his death and resurrection on our behalf, we come under the influence of God's grace. At that point, we are no longer trying to be righteous based on our own performance or perfection. We have realized that we could not save ourselves by trying to keep the law, but that we had to rely upon God's grace. The grace of God that saves us will also empower us to live victoriously in this life. This is captured in Paul's statement in Romans:

ROMANS 6:14-15
14 For sin shall not have dominion over you: for ye are not under the law, but under grace.

15 What then? Shall we sin, because we are not under the law, but under grace? God forbid.

Grace is clearly not divine permission to do wrong. Rather, it is divine empowerment to do what is right! The Christian was never intended to be a slave of sin. The law articulated God's standard, but it did not give man the power to overcome sin. It merely defined sin and revealed to man that he was a sinner.

When God's grace comes into our lives through Jesus, it not only liberates us from the penalty of sin, but it empowers us to rise victoriously above the power of sin as well. We are no longer slaves of sin! Paul explains this truth in Titus:

> **TITUS 2:11-14**
> **11 For the grace of God that brings salvation has appeared to all men,**
>
> **12 teaching us that, denying ungodliness and worldly lusts, we should live soberly, righteously, and godly in the present age,**
>
> **13 looking for the blessed hope and glorious appearing of our great God and Savior Jesus Christ,**
>
> **14 who gave himself for us, that he might redeem us from every lawless deed and purify for himself His own special people, zealous for good works.**

There is a lift that comes into our lives when we yield to the influence of God's grace. Not only do we receive salvation, but we are also taught how to live righteously. We are even directed to look up for the glorious return of the Lord Jesus. Staying *under* grace will put us *over*!

3. Stay *under* authority.

We live in a world where lawlessness and defiant, rebellious attitudes abound. Jesus speaks of the last days, saying, "Because lawlessness will abound, the love of many will grow cold" (Matt. 24:12). Peter warned of "proud and arrogant" people who "despise authority" (2 Pet. 1:10, *NLT*). Even though Paul lived in a time when governments were not necessarily favorable toward righteous causes, he advised the Roman believers to "submit to governing authorities" and to "give respect and honor to those who are in authority" (Rom. 13:1, 7, *NLT*). Paul's admonition might seem naïve to some people today, given the current attitudes we see around us, but Jesus and Peter warned us about the days in which we live.

It is important for us to remember that we are part of the Kingdom of God, and God's Kingdom operates within guidelines and principles of authority. When we align ourselves with God's system, blessing results. Matthew's gospel presents the story of the Roman centurion whose servant fell sick. The centurion tells Jesus:

MATTHEW 8:8-9
8 "Lord, I am not worthy that you should come under my roof. But only speak a word, and my servant will be healed.
9 For I also am a man under authority, having soldiers under me. And I say to this one, "Go,' and he goes; and to another, "Come,' and he comes; and to my servant, 'Do this,' and he does it."

Jesus responded to the centurion's faith and healed his servant. Jesus marveled at the centurion's faith, which was directly connected to his understanding of authority. When we align ourselves with authority, we are in a much better position to see the blessings of God flow and operate in our lives.

One way that lift can occur in our lives is when we respect and honor the spiritual authorities who are assigned to speak God's Word into our lives. The author of Hebrews advises, "Be responsive to your pastoral leaders. Listen to their counsel" (Heb. 13:17, *MSG*). Those who have wise pastors speaking the Word of God accurately and lovingly into their lives are truly blessed people. We are lifted when we receive the Word of God from godly leaders.

Some people are very rebellious. They do not want to submit to anyone. Even if they put on an outward appearance of submitting, they continue to carry inward rebellion. Pride and rebellion cause people to be at odds against all types of authority. We should respect and adhere to directives from established authorities as long as they do not contradict the teachings of the Bible. We are to obey laws and "commands" that do not lead us into illegal, unethical, or immoral activities. This kind of proper submission to civic leaders, employers, and spiritual leaders does not bring bondage. Rather, it brings blessing into the life of a believer. Staying under authority helps put us over in life!

4. Stay *under* the shadow of the Almighty.

In times of trouble, there is no safer place to be than in the perfect will of God. When situations seem threatening, the believer can look to the protection and comfort of the Holy Spirit. Remember, "The angel of the Lord encamps all around those who fear Him, and delivers them" (Psalm 34:7). Look to God! Remember His promises! Trust in Him at all times! Countless believers have turned to the Book of Psalms in seasons of difficulty and have found tremendous strength from the divinely inspired words.

PSALM 91:1-4

1 He who dwells in the secret place of the Most High shall abide under the shadow of the Almighty.

2 I will say of the Lord, "he is my refuge and my fortress; my God in him I will trust." 3 Surely he shall deliver you from the snare of the fowler, and from the perilous pestilence.

4 He shall cover you with his feathers, and under his wings you shall take refuge; his truth shall be your shield and buckler.

PSALM 17:8
8 Keep me as the apple of your eye; Hide me under the shadow of your wings.

PSALM 36:7
7 How precious is your lovingkindness, O God! Therefore the children of men put their trust under the shadow of your wings.

These passages paint a very powerful picture of God hovering over us as a mother bird would protect its young. Jesus conveyed this same imagery in his ministry as well. He said to Jerusalem, "How often I've ached to embrace your children, the way a hen gathers her chicks under her wings…" (Matt. 23:37, *MSG*). It is God's nature to provide protection, and it is God's will for us to trust and take refuge in him. We can cultivate our faith by reading, hearing, and meditating on his promises, such as the ones in the previous verses. We can also envision God hovering over us and protecting us, and we can speak confidently because of his faithfulness toward us. Staying under the shadow of the Almighty lifts our spirits and gives us great boldness in life.

5. Keep your flesh *under*.

While we need to govern our body, it is not good to see our body as an evil prison from which we must escape. Rather, we should see our body as the temple of the Holy Spirit (1 Cor. 6:19). We are to present our body "a living sacrifice, holy acceptable to God." Paul calls this our "reasonable service" (Rom. 12:1). It is important, though, to recognize that our body was never meant to rule us. Our body is designed to be our servant, not our master. Galatians chapter five reveals two routes we can take as Christians: We can yield to our flesh—our carnal nature, or we can yield to our spiritual nature. God has clearly called us to be spiritual, to be governed by the Word of God and the influence of the Holy Spirit. To do this, we must keep our body under and bring it into subjection. The following two passages of Scripture reveal how we are to perceive and govern our bodies:

1 CORINTHIANS 9:27

27 But I discipline my body and bring it into subjection, lest, when I have preached to others, I myself should become disqualified.

ROMANS 13:12-14

12 The night is far spent, the day is at hand. Therefore let us cast off the works of darkness, and let us put on the armor of light.

13 Let us walk properly, as in the day, not in revelry and drunkenness, not in lewdness and lust, not in strife and envy.

14 But put on the Lord Jesus Christ, and make no provision for the flesh, to fulfill its lusts.

The best way to keep the flesh under is not to focus on the desires and whims of the flesh, but rather, to proactively and intentionally give prominence to the rule of the Holy Spirit as he operates through our human spirit. The flesh may fight and complain, but the spiritual nature can and will prevail.

Paul reminds us, "If by the Spirit you put to death the deeds of the body, you will live" (Rom. 8:13). He tells another group of believers, "Walk in the Spirit, and you shall not fulfill the lust of the flesh" (Gal. 5:16). We don't keep our flesh under by gritting our teeth and using mere will power but by yielding to the higher influence of God's Word and Spirit. And in so doing, we position ourselves to live a higher, more fulfilling, and more victorious life.

6. Keep Satan *under* your feet.

A believer should never see himself or herself as being under Satan's power or authority. The believer is in Christ and a part of the Body of Christ. Jesus has conquered all powers and all principalities; they are all under him. Since we are in Christ, they are under us as well, and we have authority and dominion over all of Satan's power through Jesus. We can have great spiritual boldness because of Jesus, who says, "I give you the authority to trample on serpents and scorpions, and over all the power of the enemy, and nothing shall by any means hurt you" (Luke 10:19). It is important for us to remember who we are in Christ and to know our position in Christ—we have been seated with Christ in heavenly places (Eph. 2:6).

Does our victory in Christ mean that we won't face any battles? Certainly not. That is why Paul describes in great detail "the full armor of God" in Ephesians 6:10-18—so we can walk experientially in the victory that is already ours legally. When we see ourselves in Christ, when we think like those who have been raised with Christ and who share his victory, we can walk in and enjoy a higher life.

7. Stay *under* the blood.

The Apostle John tells us, "If we walk in the light as he is in the light, we have fellowship with one another, and the blood of Jesus Christ his Son cleanses us from all sin" (1 John 1:7). A person who trusts in himself, who thinks he is good enough for God on his own merits, is under condemnation (see John 3:18). However, a person who trusts in Jesus and in his shed blood has been cleansed and declared righteous before God. While forgiveness is a wonderful benefit of Jesus' redemptive work on the cross, his blood does far more than provide forgiveness. Hebrews 13:20 refers to "the blood of the everlasting covenant." God has established his covenant with us based on the blood of his Son! Forgiveness, as wonderful as it is, is simply one of many benefits of God's covenant with us.

In the Old Testament, the blood of animal sacrifices typically spoke prophetically of the blood that Jesus would ultimately shed. One such case was when the Israelites were about to be delivered from Egyptian bondage. The Israelites had been instructed to apply the blood of a lamb to the top and sides of the doorframes of their houses. Moses then instructs the people:

EXODUS 12:23
23 For the Lord will pass through to strike the Egyptians; and when he sees the blood on the lintel and on the two doorposts, the Lord will pass over the door and not allow the destroyer to come into your houses to strike you.

Ruin, death, and destruction would not come to them because the Israelites who were "under the blood."

We should never neglect to be thankful for the continual influence of the blood of Jesus Christ in our lives. A famous old song says, "There is a fountain filled with blood, drawn from Emmanuel's veins. And sinners plunged beneath that flood lose all their guilty stains." Another song reminds us that the blood shall never lose its power! While we should strive to live righteously before God, we should never fail to be thankful for the continual cleansing that is available to us through the power of Jesus' blood.

When we stay "under the blood," which means we're trusting in the power and benefits provided by the blood Jesus shed for us, not only is forgiveness and cleansing available to us, but we are also lifted into all the benefits of the covenant that God has established with us.

God wants to put us over in life! He wants us to be the head and not the tail. He wants us to be above and not beneath. However, in order for us to go over, there are some "unders" to which we must attend. We have a part to play when it comes to choosing our position in life. God has given us specific things that we can do to experience *lift* and be raised up to the level of life he wants us to enjoy.

A Resurrection Declaration

Lord, thank you for establishing the right way for me to advance and experience lift in life, a way that does not leave me with regret. Thank you that I can humble myself under your mighty hand, knowing that you will exalt me. It strengthens me to know that no one can take me from your powerful hand. Thank you that I can stay under the influence of your grace, and that your mercy, forgiveness, and empowerment flow into my life. Thank you that I can stay under authority, praying for and honoring those you've placed in my life for my benefit. I also thank you that I can stay under the shadow of the Almighty—and for the refuge and protection you extend to me there. Thank you that I can walk in the Spirit and not be ruled by my flesh. Thank you that Satan is under my feet and that you have given me authority over all the power of the enemy. And, finally, I thank you that by faith I abide under the wonderful influence of the cleansing blood of Jesus Christ. When I stay *under* in the right ways, I am perfectly positioned for you to put me *over* in every area of life. In Jesus' name, I pray—amen.

Bonus Quotes

"There is something in humility which strangely exalts the heart."

—Augustine

"God creates out of nothing. Therefore, until a man is nothing, God can make nothing out of him."

—Martin Luther

"Power is given only to those who dare to lower themselves and pick it up."

—Fyodor Dostoevsky

"If Jesus had not risen from the dead, no right-minded person would have glorified anything so hideous and repulsive as a cross stained with the blood of Jesus. An unopened grave would never have opened heaven."

—Billy Graham

"This attitude of complete submission and complete trust is of course the key to working out our own salvation in fear and trembling and is the mark of a truly spiritual Christian."

—John F. Walvoord

 Lyrics that Lift: Hymns of the Resurrection

From "Crown Him With Many Crowns" by Matthew Bridges (1851)

Crown Him the Lord of life!

Who triumphed o'er the grave,

Who rose victorious in the strife

For those He came to save.

His glories now we sing,

Who died, and rose on high,

Who died eternal life to bring,

And lives that death may die.

 Questions for Reflection and Discussion

1. There are right ways and wrong ways to excel and "get to the top" in life. Have you ever tried getting to the top the wrong way or by taking short cuts? Did you regret it later? Have you ever struggled with envy when others experienced success without going about it the right way?

2. This chapter deals with seven different "unders" that will help put us over in life. By way of review, they are:

   - Stay under the mighty hand of God.
   - Stay under grace.
   - Stay under authority.
   - Stay under the shadow of the Almighty.
   - Keep your flesh under.
   - Keep Satan under your feet.
   - Stay under the blood.

   Which of these seven seems to be the easiest for you to grasp and understand? Which of these do you feel you have the strongest inclination toward? Is there one (or more) of these that you feel is more difficult to comprehend or more challenging to do?

3. What are some appropriate ways to stay under authority? How could you apply these principles when relating to spiritual authorities? How could you live them out in relation to natural authorities? Have you seen people encounter problems in their lives due to rebellious and lawless attitudes and behaviors? What are the blessings of being properly submitted to God-ordained authority?

4. Paul advises one group of believers, "Walk in the Spirit, and you shall not fulfill the lust of the flesh" (Gal. 5:16). What does it mean to you

when you hear that we are to "keep the flesh under?" Do you think that all believers deal with the same temptations and carnal tendencies, or do you think everyone struggles in his or her own particular area? Has there ever been an area in your life where you had to really apply yourself when it came to walking in the Spirit and keeping your flesh under?

5. Review the scriptures referenced in the section "Keep Satan Under Your Feet." The verses referenced are Luke 10:19, Ephesians 2:6, and Ephesians 6:10-18. How real to you is your dominion (through Christ) over all demonic powers? Are you secure and confident in knowing that you have been raised with Christ and share in his spiritual authority? Do you believe you walk in and exercise that authority as you should?

6. Think back through the teaching in this chapter regarding the seven "unders" that will "put you over." List one thing you learned and one thing you can do right now that will allow you to begin accessing more of God's resurrection power—his *lift*—in your life.

CHAPTER TEN

Teflon™ or Velcro®? What Sticks to You, and What Slides Off?

Therefore submit to God. Resist the devil and he will flee from you.

—James 4:7

"I'm rubber. You're glue. Whatever you say bounces off me and sticks to you." Did you ever hear this defensive taunt on the playground as a kid? Rubber is bouncy and resilient. Whatever hits it bounces right off. When I was a young child "super balls" made out of very dense rubber were popular. Not only did these toys bounce extremely high, they also never lost their shape! Glue, on the other hand, is sticky, and anything that touches it tends to stay put. If we were trying to communicate this same principle with more modern technology, we might refer to Teflon™ and Velcro®.

Teflon™ is a non-stick coating often found on pans and other kinds of cookware. The promise of Teflon™ is that nothing is supposed to stick to it. Whatever is cooked on it is supposed to simply slide right off. Velcro®, on the other hand, is a nylon or polyester fastener: One side of the fabric is made of many very small hooks, and the other side is comprised of tiny loops. When the two fabrics are pressed together, they form a bond that resists separation. Pulling apart the connected fabrics results in a "ripping" sound. Velcro® often replaces many types of snaps, clasps, zippers, and even shoestrings. In short, everything slides off Teflon™, while Velcro® grabs and holds.

To use an analogy, we might say that our spiritual and emotional health depends on our knowing when to be Teflon™ and when to be Velcro®. Whether *lift* or *drag* prevails in our life depends on what slides off and what sticks. We need to be Teflon™ when it comes to the devil and carnal things. We need to know how to let negative words and worldly pressures slide off of us. With God and godly things, we need to be Velcro®. We need to let the things of God—his Word and his constructive influence—stick to us. For sake of illustration, could we paraphrase Isaiah 54:19 like this? No weapon formed against you shall prosper [it won't stick to you because you are Teflon™], and every tongue that rises against you in judgment you shall condemn. This is the heritage of the servants of the Lord, and their righteousness [which sticks to them because they are Velcro®] is from me," says the Lord.

We need to make sure that we don't get Teflon™ and Velcro® switched around. If we are Velcro® toward negative and oppressing influences and Teflon™ toward the things of God, we will only suffer.

"Teflon™ Christianity"

When Jesus was tempted (Matt. 4:1-11), none of what the enemy threw at him "stuck." Because of the life of God on the inside of him, Jesus was like Teflon™ to the temptations and distortions of truth that came against him. When scriptures were twisted and used against him, Jesus responds, "The Scriptures also say..." (Matt. 4:7, *NLT*). When encountering the Pharisees who were attacking him, Jesus says, "It is also written..." (John 8:17). Lies, falsehoods, error, and accusations can stick to people and drag them down. Jesus, though, was full of grace and truth; attacks and offenses simply did not stick to him. In John 14:30, Jesus says, "The ruler of this world is coming, and he has nothing in me." *The Message* renders this, "The chief of this godless world is about to attack. But don't worry—he has nothing on me, no claim on me."

During his ministry, no temptation or accusation of the enemy ever "stuck" to Jesus. This "non-stick" trait is not a privilege reserved for Jesus; he extended this protection to his disciples as well. Consider what Jesus tells his followers in Luke 10:19: "Behold, I give you the authority to trample on serpents and scorpions, and over all the power of the enemy, and nothing shall by any means hurt you."

This verse says that nothing shall by any means hurt us! Is that what you've been experiencing? If not, perhaps you need to focus a bit on your Teflon™-coating, so to speak (Eph. 6:10-18). In Mark's version of the Great Commission (Mark 16:15-18), Jesus speaks of certain signs that would follow believers, such as casting out demons, speaking with new tongues, and laying hands on the sick for healing. But Jesus also states, "They will take up serpents; and if they drink anything deadly, it will by no means hurt them" (16:18). Jesus was not advocating foolish practices, but he was telling his followers that as they went about doing the Father's will, there would be a provision of protection for them—the attacks of the enemy wouldn't stick!

In Acts chapter 20, Paul speaks of the challenges that he knew were ahead of him. He even refers to "chains and tribulations" that he would face. But then he says, "But none of these things move me" (v. 24). In other words, Paul realizes that while he would experience some of these things, they wouldn't stick! When the viper bit him (Acts 28:3), he shook it off into the fire and felt no harm. Was it pleasant to be bit by a snake? I'm sure it wasn't. And it's not necessarily pleasant to deal with some of the hardships, pressures, and challenges that we face in life. But the point is that there was a greater power at work in the life of Jesus and the life of Paul—greater than the power that was released against them. That same power—the power of God's life and God's Spirit—is available to us today. We can walk in that power, and it can work mightily in us.

"Velcro® Christianity"

When we speak of Velcro® Christianity, we're talking about having an aggressive attitude toward the things of God—a tenacity that seizes upon what God has said and refuses to let go. In Luke 8:15, Jesus speaks of the kind of person who brings forth fruit from the Word: "But the seed in the good earth—these are the good-hearts who seize the Word and hold on no matter what, sticking with it until there is a harvest" (*MSG*). That is a Velcro® attitude!

Eleazar is an Old Testament figure who possessed a Velcro® attitude toward his assignment from God. When God's people were attacked, everyone retreated. Everyone but Eleazar. This man "stood his ground and killed Philistines right and left until he was exhausted—but he never let go of his sword! A big win for God that day" (2 Sam. 23:10, *MSG*). The *New King James Version* says that Eleazar's "hand stuck to the sword."

Here is a great principle: If you'll stick to the Sword, the Sword will stick to you! Eleazar didn't just stick to his sword; he also stuck to his assignment. He was like Velcro® when it came to the Word of God and the plan of God for his life.

The believers who received the Book of Hebrews in the New Testament were experiencing an unfortunate reversal. They were in the process of becoming Teflon™ when they should have been Velcro® and vice versa (at least they were being tempted in that direction). They were letting slip the promises that should have been sticking! And the pressures they should have been letting slide were sticking. Consider these passages about what was slipping and what was sticking:

HEBREWS 2:1 (*KJV*)
1 Therefore we ought to give the more earnest heed to the things which we have heard, lest at any time we should let them slip.

HEBREWS 3:6
6 But Christ as a Son over his own house, whose house we are if we hold fast the confidence and the rejoicing of the hope firm to the end.

HEBREWS 3:14
14 For we have become partakers of Christ if we hold the beginning of our confidence steadfast to the end....

HEBREWS 10:35-36
35 Therefore do not cast away your confidence, which has great reward.

36 For you have need of endurance, so that after you have done the will of God, you may receive the promise....

These passages indicate a strong need for us to endure—and to hold tight to the confidence we have in Christ and his finished work. If we hold fast to Jesus' teachings and God's established principles, we can rest assured that our hope will not disappoint us: We will receive what God has promised.

A Time for Teflon™ and a Time for Velcro®

Shadrach, Meshach, and Abednego are examples of individuals who knew when to be Velcro® and when to be Teflon™. When threatened, they were Velcro® regarding their trust, confidence, and consecration toward God. However, concerning the threats of the king, they were Teflon™—they let his menacing, intimidating words slide right off.

DANIEL 3:17-18
17 Our God whom we serve is able to deliver us from the burning fiery furnace, and he will deliver us from your hand, O king.

18 But if not, let it be known to you, O king, that we do not serve your gods, nor will we worship the gold image which you have set up.

This is an example of Velcro®—a tenacious clinging to the faithfulness of God—and because of their Velcro® toward the things of God, they had, as it were, a Teflon™ coating that protected them from what would have destroyed them. Even though Nebuchadnezzar had all three men thrown into the fire, they were untouched.

DANIEL 3:27

27 They saw these men on whose bodies the fire had no power; the hair of their head was not singed nor were their garments affected, and the smell of fire was not on them.

When it comes to the things we have received—the Word of God and our confidence—we cannot let them slip away and slide off of us. We must be like Velcro®. We must stick to some things and let some things stick to us! However, when it comes to the pressures and problems of the world, we need to develop some Teflon™ tendencies—we need to let *those* things roll off of us, as we cast every care upon the Lord (1 Pet. 5:7).

A Resurrection Declaration

Lord, I choose to submit to you and to resist the devil. Thank you for helping me to be a person who lays hold of your Word and tenaciously holds on to it. I treasure every promise and every commandment in your Word. Whatever your Spirit says to me, I want to hold it firmly and allow it to take deep root within me, knowing it will produce the fruit in me that you desire. I also want to be a person who repels and resists the enemy's words and influence. I believe with all of my heart that no weapon formed against me will prosper. The righteousness I possess is from you. I thank you that you have given me authority over all of the power of the enemy and that nothing shall by any means hurt me. Thank you for helping me to be like Teflon™ toward everything from the enemy, and for helping me to be like Velcro® concerning you and all of the good things you have for me. In Jesus' name, I pray—amen.

Bonus Quotes

"We conquer, not in any brilliant fashion—we conquer by continuing."

—George Matheson

"God knows what each one of us is dealing with. He knows our pressures. He knows our conflicts. And He has made a provision for each and every one of them. That provision is Himself in the person of the Holy Spirit, indwelling us and empowering us to respond rightly."

—Kay Arthur

"Through many dangers, toils and snares, I have already come;
'Tis grace hath brought me safe thus far,
and grace will lead me home."

—John Newton (Amazing Grace)

"Endurance is not just the ability to bear a hard thing, but to turn it into glory."

—William Barclay

"Learn to say 'no' to the good so you can say 'yes' to the best."

—John Maxwell

Lyrics that Lift: Hymns of the Resurrection

From "All Ye That Seek the Lord Who Died" by Charles Wesley (1746)

Go tell the followers of your Lord
Their Jesus is to life restored;
He lives, that they His life may find;
He lives, to quicken all mankind.

Questions for Reflection and Discussion

1. How is your spiritual "Teflon™ coating" working? Are you able to deflect discouragement and unjust criticisms? Are you staying free from offense, bitterness, and unforgiveness? Have you released pain from your past so that it won't hinder your future?
2. How did Jesus use Scripture in order to be like Teflon™, so to speak?
3. How are you doing when it comes to being like Velcro®? Do you grasp spiritual principles and retain biblical truth? What do you do keep yourself reinforced and reminded so that the right things stick to you?
4. Eleazar is an amazing example of someone who demonstrated Velcro®-like tenacity and endurance in his life. He did not quit and refused to give up. Is there someone you can think of who has continued faithfully for a long period of time without giving up? What are the benefits of their endurance in their work? Without naming names, do you know others who never stick with anything very long and are always

bouncing from one thing to another? What are the problems created by that kind of short-term, erratic behavior?

5. Review the four passages in the Book of Hebrews (2:1, 3:6, 14; 10:35-36). What indication do these verses give us about the significance and importance of endurance, perseverance, and tenacity in the life of the believer?

6. Think back through the teaching in this chapter regarding the idea of things sticking to you or sliding off. List one thing you learned and one thing you can do right now that will allow you to begin accessing more of God's resurrection power—his *lift*—in your life.

CHAPTER ELEVEN

Navigating the Hills, Plains, and Valleys

"There is not a square inch in the whole domain of our human existence over which Christ, who is Sovereign over all, does not cry, Mine!"

—Abraham Kuyper

In the Old Testament, the enemies of Israel made a serious miscalculation. Having lost a battle against the Israelites, the advisors to the King of Syria said, "Their gods are gods of the hills. Therefore they were stronger than we; but if we fight against them in the plain, surely we will be stronger than they" (1 Kings 20:23). It was a common belief in heathen lands that gods were territorial in nature (the god of a river, the god of a forest, the god of a city, and so forth) and that their influence was restricted to their particular territory. Because of this misguided thinking, the Syrians had the idea that Israel's God was a territorial god, that he was restricted in his ability to deliver his people. They perceived Israel's God to like all other gods. In other words, they assumed him limited in range, influence, ability, and power.

As a result of their erroneous thinking, the Syrians developed a new strategy that they thought would be successful: They decided to fight the Israelites where (they thought) Israel's God could not help them. But God had a surprise in store for the Syrians: "Then a man of God came and spoke to the king of Israel, and said, 'Thus says the Lord: "Because the Syrians have said, 'The Lord is God of the hills, but he is not God of the valleys,' therefore I will deliver all this great multitude into your hand, and you shall know that I am the Lord" (1 Kings 20:28). God wanted everyone to know that he was not limited and restricted (as the Syrians thought). He is not just the God of the hills, but he is the God of the plains and valleys as well!

If we want to speak of God's power in a territorial or geographical sense, we should remember that Abraham says God is "the Possessor of heaven and earth." (Gen. 14:22). David writes, "The earth is the Lord's, and all its fullness, the world and those who dwell therein" (Psalm 24:1). God says through the prophet Isaiah, "Heaven is my throne, and earth is my footstool" (Isa. 66:1). The point here is not that God owns a lot of real estate, but that God's reign over creation is comprehensive and supreme. He really is *the Lord*, and he wants to reign supreme in every area and dimension of our lives. He doesn't just want to be Lord of our religious life or church life. He wants to govern and influence us in *every* area of life—our social life, our personal life, our thought life, our financial life, and our family life. He wants to reign supreme in our vocation, our health, and our habits.

The Syrians wanted to "compartmentalize" God and assign him a limited, restricted role in Israel's existence, but God was not going to have it. The enemy thought that Israel's God was only a God of the hills, but God wants us to know that he is the God of the hills, the plains, and the valleys! Let's look at what it means for God to rule in these three areas of our lives.

The God of the Hills

Naturally speaking, high levels of success are described with phrases such as "on top of the world," "the pinnacle of success," and "peak performance." Spiritually speaking, "hills" can refer to the high points in our lives, the times when we feel like we're on top of the world. Sometimes people refer to these as "mountaintop experiences." For many, such encounters with the Lord become landmarks and milestones in their lives—these moments can launch people into a life-long spiritual journey. God strategically uses mountains throughout Scripture, sometimes relating to times of visitation and revelation when God's glory is poured out in a special way. Consider these mountaintop experiences:

- God revealed himself to Abraham as Jehovah Jireh on Mount Moriah.
- God gave the Law to Moses on Mount Sinai.
- God spoke to Elijah in a still, small voice on Mount Horeb.

In his earthly life, Jesus achieved victory over the greatest temptations while on a mountain; his most glorious moment was on the Mount of Transfiguration; and he ascended from the Mount of Olives.

Clearly, mountaintop experiences get our attention, and people understandably desire to have these kinds of experiences. A word of caution, though, is in order when it comes to mountaintops. If a person is not careful, he can get the idea that the chief aim of life is to have a non-stop euphoric experience. Peter was privileged to observe Jesus, Moses, and Elijah interacting on the Mount of Transfiguration. Peter enjoyed a truly glorious experience, seeing Jesus in his transfigured state, with his face as radiant as the sun and his clothes a brilliant white (Matt. 17:2). What was Peter's reaction to this remarkable experience? Peter tried to make the moment last forever, saying, "Lord, it is good for us to be here; if you wish, let us make here three tabernacles: one for you, one for Moses, and one for Elijah" (Matt. 17:4).

I can understand the desire to set up camp and linger indefinitely around a glorious experience, but that was not God's will. Jesus descended from the mountain and directly ministered deliverance to a boy suffering from epilepsy (Matt. 17:1-4). Had Jesus stayed on the mountaintop, he would not have been able to reach people where they were. This reminds me of a story involving the great evangelist Dwight L. Moody. Warren Wiersbe writes:

> A man once testified in one of D.L. Moody's meetings that he had lived "on the Mount of Transfiguration" for five years.
>
> "How many souls did you lead to Christ last year?" Moody bluntly asked him.
>
> "Well," the man hesitated, "I don't know."
>
> "Have you saved any?" Moody persisted.
>
> "I don't know that I have," the man admitted.
>
> "Well," said Moody, "we don't want that kind of mountaintop experience. When a man gets up so high that he cannot reach down and save poor sinners, there is something wrong."[26]

[26] Warren Wiersbe, *The Wycliffe Handbook of Preaching and Preachers* (Chicago: Moody Press, 1984), 202.

Mountaintop experiences were not meant to be permanent but were meant to be times of illumination and impartation, enabling us to be more effective ministers to people when we meet them where they are.

Another issue to watch out for when it comes to mountaintops is the danger of getting into pride. When people ascend to success, they sometimes lose their humility and become arrogant. Uzziah, one of the kings in the Old Testament, is a sad testimony to this tendency. Consider the chain of events detailed in Second Chronicles:

- Uzziah sought God (26:5).
- As long as he sought the Lord, God made him prosper (26:5).
- God helped him (26:7).
- His fame spread…he became exceedingly strong (26:8).
- Great accomplishments are reported (26:9-14).
- His fame spread far and wide, for he was marvelously helped until he became strong (26:15).

All of this sounds like outstanding trajectory, but once he becomes strong, Uzziah seems to forget God and no longer seek him. Scripture proceeds to detail his downfall:

2 CHRONICLES 2:16 (*MSG*)
16 But then the strength and success went to his head. Arrogant and proud, he fell. One day, contemptuous of God, he walked into The Temple of God like he owned it and took over, burning incense on the Incense Altar.

God wants to lift us and help us accomplish his will, but we must not forget God when we experience success. We need to stay humble, and we need to be willing to "step down" from whatever success we enjoy in order to continue helping others. When we experience God's blessings, we will be well served to remember Paul's advice: "Don't be stuck-up. Make friends with nobodies; don't be the great somebody" (Rom. 12:16, *MSG*).

The God of the Plains

When you consider all of the scriptures about God lifting his people, it's easy to relate to the idea of God being the God of the hills. But God isn't just with us when we are on top of everything. He is also the God of the plains. Figuratively speaking, "the plains" refer to what we consider the routine, ordinary, day-to-day aspects of our lives. Some of the connotations of the word "plain" include *simple*, *not fancy*, *ordinary*, *routine*, and *mundane*. When looking at the map of the United States, there are areas we refer to as "the plains." These are typically not exciting places to drive through because the landscape lacks variation. However, this part of the nation is where much of our food and sources of energy come from. Similarly, much of the Church's productivity comes from "plain" Christians and ministries.

Society conditions us to overlook the plain things of life—rarely do we fully appreciate the simple and the ordinary. Instead, we tend to focus on the razzle-dazzle, the spectacular, and the sensational. The grass looks greener on the other side, and we are more impressed by the sizzle, so to speak, than the steak. Because of these tendencies, people often become impatient, lack contentment, and become thrill-seekers. People do not know how to handle something when the newness of it wears off, when the honeymoon period is over, or when the goosebumps subside.

God is just as interested in our life's plains as he is in our life's hills! Steady walking across the plains may not seem as euphoric as reaching a mountaintop, but important business takes place in the plains. The plains are where we demonstrate consistency and discipline, and it is where we establish stability in our lives. If our lungs could speak, they might say that the function they perform (breathing air in, breathing air out—over and over again) is not as exciting as what the eyes do (seeing the world! Sunsets, beauty, loved ones…) or what the tongue does (tasting all kinds of delicious foods), but what the lungs do is essential! "Air in" and "air out" may seem more mundane than exhilarating, but without this constant exchange of oxygen and carbon dioxide, our bodies would quickly die.

Discontentment can be a challenge, especially when we compare ourselves to others. Have you ever found yourself thinking any of the following thoughts?

- *Who you are and what you are doing is insignificant because you are not a missionary or a pastor. What you do for God does not matter.*
- *Your marriage is not as exciting as the relationships you see on television and in the movies. You need to go out and find someone else.*
- *Your church is no longer exciting. You need to find a new church.*
- *What you are doing as a* ________________________ [fill in the blank with your vocation or calling] *is not as important as what So-and-so is doing.*

The Apostle Paul shares his wisdom with us, saying, "I have learned in whatever state I am, to be content" (Phil. 4:11). Scripture also directs, "Be content with such things as you have" (Heb. 13:5). There is nothing wrong with improving or advancing in life in appropriate and godly ways—that is a good thing—but we shouldn't let ourselves be motivated by comparison, insecurity, impatience, or any other misguided factor.

We achieve both natural and spiritual success by consistently doing the right things—not because they are thrilling, but because they are necessary. We can experience lift even in the plains! God is pleased when we faithfully and diligently carry out our basic responsibilities, and the Holy Spirit will strengthen, enable, and empower us as we do the things this life requires us to do.

The God of the Valleys

And what about the valleys? Everyone knows what they are: The valleys represent the low times, the difficult times, the challenging times, the seasons of trial or sorrow. Thank God that he is with us through the valleys and does not abandon us when we hit hard times. Always remember what Psalm 23:4 says: "Yea, though I walk through the valley of the shadow of death, I will fear no evil; for you are with me." Notice the emphasis on walking *through* the valley—not setting up camp in the valley. "If you're going through hell, keep going," a popular phrase often attributed to Winston Churchill, accurately captures the attitude we must embrace when facing difficulty.

The Apostle Paul wisely states, "Our present troubles are small and won't last very long." Paul sees current problems in the larger context of "a glory that vastly outweighs them and will last forever" (2 Cor. 4:17, *NLT*). When we keep our eyes on the goodness, greatness, and faithfulness of God, it is possible to go through the valley and emerge *lifted* on the other side. To experience this lift, we must maintain hope. Without hope, we can lose sight of what is ahead. King David knows a thing or two about the power of hope. In peril numerous times throughout his life, David is described as "the man raised up on high" (2 Sam. 23:1). He writes, "Be of good courage, and He shall strengthen your heart, all you who hope in the Lord" (Ps. 31:24).

If you happen to be going through a valley right now, here are some powerful scriptures that will help you maintain hope. Meditate on these verses (emphases mine) about the lifting and rescuing nature of God.

PSALM 9:13

13 Have mercy on me, O Lord! Consider my trouble from those who hate me, you who *lift* me up from the gates of death.

PSALM 18:48

48 He delivers me from my enemies. You also *lift* me up above those who rise against me.

PSALM 30:1

1 I will extol You, O Lord, for you have *lifted* me up, and have not let my foes rejoice over me.

PSALM 40:2 (*NLT*)

2 He *lifted* me out of the pit of despair, out of the mud and the mire. He set my feet on solid ground and steadied me as I walked along.

PSALM 113:7-8 (*NLT*)

7 He *lifts* the poor from the dust and the needy from the garbage dump.

8 He sets them among princes, even the princes of his own people!

PSALM 145:14 (*NLT*)

14 The Lord helps the fallen and *lifts* those bent beneath their loads.

PSALM 146:8 (*NLT*)

8 The Lord opens the eyes of the blind. The Lord *lifts* up those who are weighed down. The Lord loves the godly.

In the difficult times, we can be tempted to feel that God is no longer with us. Focus for a moment, if you will, on the letters N-O-W-H-E-R-E. What word did you see when you looked at the letters? Some people will see the word "nowhere," but others will see the words "now" "here." Remember—no matter what you're going through, God is *now here* with you! God is not just the God of the hills; our God is the God of the hills, plains, and valleys. He is God everywhere, at all times, during all seasons. And even though there is coming a day in the future when we will receive a transformed, glorified body, God is *now here*, calling us to live a resurrection-empowered life *here* and *now*!

! A Resurrection Declaration

Lord, I thank you that you are not just the God of the hills, plains, and valleys, but you are also the Most High God, the God of heaven and earth. You are the God over all creation, and you are the God over every part of my life. I surrender myself to your Lordship—the entirety of who I am and what I do. Thank you for the success and victory that you have brought into my life. I acknowledge that you are the source of every good and perfect gift. Help me never to forget you or fail to give you glory for every benefit and blessing that I experience in life. I also thank you for helping me to be faithful and steadfast during the routine day-to-day experiences of my life. Help me not be weary in well doing or to become disillusioned by comparing myself to other people. I resolve to be faithful in all things. Finally, thank you that I have the wonderful promise of your abiding presence in my life even through the valleys and challenging times that come. I take comfort in knowing that you will never leave me or forsake me, and that you have promised to see me through whatever adversity may come my way. Thank you for being the God of the hills, the plains, and the valleys. In Jesus' name, I pray—amen.

Bonus Quotes

"The real tragedy is the tragedy of the man who never in his life braces himself for his one supreme effort, who never stretches to his full capacity, never stands up to his full stature."

—Arnold Bennett

"Christians are not so much in danger when they are persecuted as when they are admired."

—Charles Spurgeon

"Nearly all men can stand adversity, but if you want to test a man's character, give him power."

—Abraham Lincoln

"No matter how devastating our struggles, disappointments, and troubles are, they are only temporary. No matter what happens to you, no matter the depth of tragedy or pain you face, no matter how death stalks you and your loved ones, the Resurrection promises you a future of immeasurable good."

—Josh McDowell

"Success is the sum of small efforts, repeated day in and day out."

-Robert Collier

 Lyrics that Lift: Hymns of the Resurrection

From "Awake and Sing" by Alice J. Cleator (1900)

No longer death has cruel sway;
A light surrounds the grave!
All hail the joy of Easter day;
The Lord is strong to save!

Awake, O heart, the morn is bright,
All doubt and fear is o'er!
The Lord is ris'n in power and might,
He lives forevermore!

 Questions for Reflection and Discussion

1. Do you tend to associate God with one landscape (hills, plains, or valleys) more than another? For example, have you ever felt that God was with you on a mountaintop or that he had abandoned you in a valley?
2. To what extent do you believe that God is with you no matter what "level" of life's landscape you're currently facing?
3. Consider your own history. How well have you managed the mountaintop experiences? The plains? The valleys? Are there instructions in this chapter that you think may help you navigate these levels better in the future? If so, what will you do differently?

4. Consider the example of the lungs (air in, air out). Their function does not seem exciting, but it is absolutely essential. What kinds of things in your life are like that? What do you do that may not be exciting but is important? What about someone else? Can you think of someone whose work you take for granted that you should thank and appreciate instead?
5. Review the seven references to *lift* mentioned in the various Psalms listed toward the end of this chapter. It is good to know that God lifted the psalmist out of his problems, but how ingrained are these same promises into *your* belief system to encourage you in your *own* life? Are you convinced of and comforted by God's lifting nature toward you?
6. Think back through the teaching in this chapter about navigating the hills, plains, and valleys. List one thing you learned and one thing you can do right now that will allow you to begin accessing more of God's resurrection power—his *lift*—in your life.

CHAPTER TWELVE

Wake Up! Look Up! Rise Up!

Awake, you who sleep,
Arise from the dead,
And Christ will give you light.
—Ephesians 5:14

Many people, Christians and non-Christians alike, know the story of the prodigal son—the young man who left home and messed up his life but was ultimately restored to his father's love (Luke 15:11-24). Greed, carnality, and impulsive behavior took him to the lowest experience of his life. There, in the midst of hunger and suffering, something happened.

LUKE 15:17-20 (*ESV*)
17 "But when he came to himself, he said, 'How many of my father's hired servants have more than enough bread, but I perish here with hunger!

18 I will arise and go to my father, and I will say to him, "Father, I have sinned against heaven and before you.

19 I am no longer worthy to be called your son. Treat me as one of your hired servants.'"

20 And he arose and came to his father...

The father's compassionate response to his son's return is legendary—how the father ran out to meet him, embraced him, and restored him. What an amazing portrayal of the heavenly Father's love. There is much to be said about this father's love and all that he did for his son, but for the sake of this book's focus, I want to look at three things the wayward son did that were key to his returning home: 1) He woke up; 2) he looked up; and 3) he rose up.

Wake Up!

These three elements are so vital, and they establish a pattern for everyone who wants to end up in the right spot, no matter how far off track they have gotten in the meantime. First, a person must wake up. The prodigal "came to himself" (Luke 15:17). Several other translations refer to this as him having "come to his senses." In other words, there was an awakening. Interestingly, Jesus' top three disciples—Peter, James, and John—slept through two of the most dynamic experiences that happened right in front of them: Jesus on the Mount of Transfiguration and Jesus in the Garden of Gethsemane. Imagine how much more they might have absorbed had they stayed awake and alert during those monumental moments! There are many instances in Scripture expressing God's desire for his people to be awake, alert, stirred, and attentive.

ISAIAH 50:4 (*NET*)
4 He wakes me up every morning; he makes me alert so I can listen attentively as disciples do.

JOEL 3:9
9 Wake up the mighty men…

ROMANS 13:11 (*NLT*)
11 This is all the more urgent, for you know how late it is; time is running out. Wake up, for our salvation is nearer now than when we first believed.

EPHESIANS 5:13 (*NLT*)
13 The light makes everything visible. This is why it is said, "Awake, O sleeper, rise up from the dead, and Christ will give you light."

Are we awake and alert to who God is and what he's doing in our lives? Are we actively listening to what he is saying to us?

Look Up!

The prodigal had a choice. He could keep looking down at pig slop, or he could start looking up at his father's love. There is a famous saying, "Two men looked out from prison bars—one saw the mud; the other saw the stars." When the wayward son recalled the good treatment that his father's servants received, he began to imagine a better life than the one he was experiencing. He wasn't merely remembering what he knew to be true, that his father was kind to the servants; he was beginning to see potential for *his own life*—he was beginning to look up. He wasn't only looking back at what he had in the past, but he was also looking ahead to what he could have in the future. If you are going to make progress, spiritual or otherwise, you must *look up*. You must be able to see something better—something above where you are right now.

The ability to see something before it comes to pass is integral to hope and faith. People are seldom inspired without first seeing a purpose and knowing a desirable outcome will result from their actions. Antoine De Saint-Exupery states, "A rock pile ceases to be a rock pile the moment a single man contemplates it, bearing within him the image of a cathedral." A mental picture of a desired outcome can challenge an individual, summoning from within him an empowerment that can bring about the seemingly impossible. When Abram and Sarah were barren, and there was no way in the natural they could have a child, God challenged them to look up:

> **GENESIS 13:14-15**
> **14 And the Lord said to Abram, after Lot had separated from him: "Lift your eyes now and look from the place where you are—northward, southward, eastward, and westward;**
>
> **15 for all the land which you see I give to you and your descendants forever."**

> **GENESIS 15:5**
> **5 Then he brought him outside and said, "Look now toward heaven, and count the stars if you are able to number them." And he said to him, "So shall your descendants be."**

God was really saying, "What you see is what you get." God wants to stretch your vision. God has more for you and better for you than you can imagine.

The prodigal son didn't necessarily see himself being restored to all of the privileges of sonship, but he could see himself being treated as one of his father's servants. He received much more than that! And *our* Father is able to do exceeding abundantly above all that we could ask or think (Eph. 3:20)! We serve a God whose ways and thoughts are higher than ours (Isa. 55:8-9)! If we can *see something* and act upon it, God can expand it and increase it, but we need to *see something* that gets us thinking, believing, and acting in the right direction.

Jesus told his disciples to *look up* on two particular occasions. First, after Jesus described dramatic events, he admonishes his disciples, "Now when these things begin to happen, *look up and lift up your heads*, because your redemption draws near" (Luke 21:28, emphasis mine). While Jesus may have been speaking about specific eschatological events, I believe the principle has broad application. Whenever you are facing any adversity or calamity, it is always good to look up and lift up your head! Our Redeemer is always near—he is always close to us. He is faithful, and he will never abandon us.

Another time that Jesus told his disciples to look up involves the harvest of souls that God desires to reap from the earth. Jesus states, "Do you not say, 'There are still four months and then comes the harvest'? Behold, I say to you, *lift up your eyes and look* at the fields, for they are already white for harvest!" (John 4:35, emphasis mine). How easy it is to get preoccupied with and distracted by the affairs of life and fail to see the people and needs around us. We can also procrastinate and think we will serve God later, but Jesus wants us to look up and see the potential that is in front of us at this moment.

What we look at is important! I have noticed that if I look at something on the side of the road while I'm driving, I tend to drift in that direction. If we want to go straight, it is important that we keep our eyes straight ahead. We tend to gravitate in the direction of our gaze. In the Old Testament, Abraham's nephew Lot ended up in the evil city of Sodom. Before he actually arrived at that destination, he had "lifted up his eyes, and beheld all the plain of Jordan," and, having moved that direction, he then "pitched his tent toward Sodom" (Gen. 13:10-12, *KJV*). People move toward whatever they have fixed their eyes upon.

Similarly, Eve did not arbitrarily partake of the forbidden fruit; there was a process that involved her focus. Genesis 3:6 states, "So when the woman saw that the tree was good for food, that it was pleasant to the eyes, and a tree desirable to make one wise, she took of its fruit and ate." Note that she did not *act* wrongly until she *perceived* wrongly. She "saw" certain things about the forbidden tree and fruit, but her perception was distorted. False perception is what deception is all about. That is why it is so important for us to see the right things and to believe the right things about what we see.

Throughout Scripture, we are constantly encouraged and instructed to look to God:

> **ISAIAH 45:22**
> **22 Look to me, and be saved.**
>
> **PSALM 34:5**
> **5 Those who look to him for help will be radiant with joy.**
>
> **PSALM 57:1 (*NLT*)**
> **1 I look to you for protection.**
>
> **COLOSSIANS 3:2 (*MSG*)**
> **2 Don't shuffle along, eyes to the ground, absorbed with the things right in front of you. Look up, and be alert to what is going on around Christ—that's where the action is. See things from his perspective.**

TITUS 2:13

13 Looking for the blessed hope and glorious appearing of our great God and Savior Jesus Christ…

HEBREWS 12:2

2 Looking unto Jesus, the author and finisher of our faith…

What we look at is important in our journey. We are warned in Scripture about Lot's wife who looked back (Luke 17:32). Jesus warned of the sad dilemma of the one who puts his hand to the plow and then looks back (Luke 9:62). In contrast, Proverbs 4:25 admonishes, "Look straight ahead, and fix your eyes on what lies before you" (*NLT*). What we look at—focus on, meditate on, concentrate on, dwell on—is important! Because what we look at determines our direction.

Rise Up!

It is great that the prodigal son came to his senses and awakened to the reality of the ugliness of his plight. It is also great that he began to think about and envision how much better his father's servants lived compared to what he was experiencing. But waking up and looking up don't really help a person unless he takes the third, necessary step: He must *rise up*!

The prodigal had to take the step described in Luke 15:18, which says, "I will arise and go to my father" (*ESV*). All the awareness and accurate perception in the world do not help us get where we want to be unless we also take action. The prodigal did just what he said—he arose and went to his father. This simple step combined with his repentant heart brought him in contact with the fullness of the father's love and compassion.

It is important to understand that a perfect past is not a prerequisite to experiencing future elevation. If it were, none of us would qualify. Scripture states, “The godly may trip seven times, but they will get up again” (Prov. 24:16, *NLT*). We may hate our sins and mistakes, but we must not remain in them. We must love the blood of Jesus and the plan of God more, and we must certainly not wallow in the guilt and condemnation of the past. The instructions of the Apostle John are so powerful in this regard. He writes:

> **1 JOHN 1:8–2:2 (*NLT*)**
>
> **8 If we claim we have no sin, we are only fooling ourselves and not living in the truth.**
>
> **9 But if we confess our sins to him, he is faithful and just to forgive us our sins and to cleanse us from all wickedness.**
>
> **10 If we claim we have not sinned, we are calling God a liar and showing that his word has no place in our hearts.**
>
> **1 My dear children, I am writing this to you so that you will not sin. But if anyone does sin, we have an advocate who pleads our case before the Father. He is Jesus Christ, the one who is truly righteous.**
>
> **2 He himself is the sacrifice that atones for our sins—and not only our sins but the sins of all the world.**

If we have messed up, we need to ’fess up, get up, and continue walking with God. We need to stop beating ourselves up over the past and be thankful that God has made provision for us to continue in our journey without guilt and condemnation. We are forgiven and free because of Jesus’ wonderful blood.

We can be confident about rising up, even in spite of the past, because God is constantly raising people up. That is his nature, and that is our destiny. Consider this beautiful description: “But those who wait for the Lord’s help find renewed strength; they rise up as if they had eagles’ wings, they run without growing weary, they walk without getting tired" (Isa. 40:31, *NET*).

When we cooperate with God, yielding to him and obeying him, we receive divine elevation and empowerment in our lives. He lifts us and strengthens us so that we can live a resurrected life.

In the first chapter of this book, I addressed the future resurrection of our bodies—when God raises our bodies up to be immortal and incorruptible. That will be the ultimate "rising up" for us. However, not all of our arising will happen in a future era. We can engage in some "arising" while we are still in these mortal bodies. The prodigal *arose* when he saw a preferable future and took action.

Previously in this chapter, we read how God told Abraham to lift up his eyes, to see the land in all directions, and how God told him to look to the heavens and consider the innumerable stars (Gen. 13:14-15; 15:5). God wasn't just getting Abraham to awaken to amazing potential and to envision what could be—to wake up and to look up—but God had an additional step for Abraham: "Arise, walk in the land through its length and its width, for I give it to you" (Gen. 13:17). Perception is one thing; taking possession is another. Abraham, our father in faith, had to arise and walk throughout the land that he would inherit.

Not only did Abraham and the prodigal son arise, so did four leprous men in a desperate situation. In the Old Testament, there was a time when the Syrian army had completely encircled the city of Samaria. Four lepers sat at the city gate in a seemingly impossible situation. Inside the city was a great famine, outside the city was a besieging army. Talk about being stuck between a rock and a hard place!

Realizing there was no benefit to sitting there and dying of starvation, they took a calculated risk. Second Kings 7:5 states, "They rose at twilight to go to the camp of the Syrians." When they got to the Syrian camp, they found it abandoned—God had caused the Syrians to hear what sounded to them like an approaching army and they had fled, but they left all of their food, clothes, and treasures. These four leprous men found more provision than they could have ever imagined, and it happened because they "rose at twilight." God performed a miracle on their behalf, but God's miracle didn't happen until they arose. And they arose by acting on a glimmer of hope and the belief that something good might happen.

This kind of faith and hope can fill our hearts and compel us to act—to arise. This *lift* is found in numerous passages throughout God's Word:

PSALM 20:7-8 (*ESV*)

7 Some trust in chariots and some in horses, but we trust in the name of the Lord our God.

8 They collapse and fall, but we rise and stand upright.

ISAIAH 60:1

1 Arise, shine; For your light has come! And the glory of the Lord is risen upon you.

MICAH 7:8 (*NLT*)

8 Do not gloat over me, my enemies! For though I fall, I will rise again. Though I sit in darkness, the Lord will be my light.

As we listen to God and yield to his influence, he will help us wake up, look up, and rise up. This is completely in accordance to the working of his Spirit—the same Spirit who raised Jesus from the dead and who lifts us up as well.

A Resurrection Declaration

Lord, thank you that you've given me the ability to wake up, look up, and rise up! I choose to wake up today to all of the glorious realities that you've placed in front of me, to look up at all the possibilities and promises with which you've surrounded me, and to rise up into the fullness of your plan and purpose for my life. I choose to see you today, Lord, for who you are. You are compassionate, merciful, kind, and gracious. I choose to see Satan for who he is—a defeated and vanquished foe, and one who has no power over me. I choose to see myself for who I am. I am totally forgiven, redeemed, purchased, accepted, cleansed, and righteous. God, you are who your Word says you are, and I am who your Word says I am. Thank you for empowering me to be spiritually alert, supernaturally focused, and dynamically activated to walk in these truths. I wake up, look up, and rise up for your glory. In Jesus' name, I pray—amen.

Bonus Quotes

"A proud man is always looking down on things and people; and, of course, as long as you are looking down, you cannot see something that is above you."

—C. S. Lewis

"When one door closes another door opens, but we so often look so long and so regretfully upon the closed door that we do not see the ones which open for us."

—Alexander Graham Bell

"The vision must be followed by the venture. It is not enough to stare up the steps—we must step up the stairs."

—Vance Havner

"Look outside, be distressed.
Look inside, be depressed.
Look at Jesus, be at rest."

—Corrie Ten Boom

Saint Patrick's Breastplate (An Irish Prayer from the Eighth Century)

"I rise today
with the power of God to pilot me,
God's strength to sustain me,
God's wisdom to guide me,
God's eye to look ahead for me,
God's ear to hear me,
God's word to speak for me,
God's hand to protect me,
God's way before me,
God's shield to defend me,
God's host to deliver me,
From snares of devils,
From evil temptations,
From nature's failings,
From all who wish to harm me,
Far or near,
Alone and in a crowd."

 Lyrics that Lift: Hymns of the Resurrection

From "Christ Arose" by Robert Lowry (1874)

Low in the grave He lay,
Jesus, my Savior,
Waiting the coming day,
Jesus, my Lord!

Up from the grave He arose,
With a mighty triumph o'er His foes,
He arose a Victor from the dark domain,
And He lives forever, with His saints to reign.
He arose! He arose!
Hallelujah! Christ arose!

 Questions for Reflection and Discussion

1. The prodigal son experienced what could be called "a rude awakening" when the consequences of his wrong choices fully manifested. Have you ever experienced a rude awakening of some kind? Have you ever seen someone else go through this? What were the results?
2. Unlike having to be awakened from blatant sin, have you ever simply awakened to realities that you had not been paying attention to? How did God get your attention, and what was the realization you came to? What did you do once you "saw" what you needed to see?

3. We read the following quote in this chapter: "Two men looked out from prison bars—one saw the mud; the other saw the stars." Have you experienced either the negative or the positive aspects of this quote? Have you seen "mud" or "stars" solely because of the way you chose to look at certain situations? Is there any area right now in which you are unnecessarily focusing on the mud, so to speak?

4. Do you agree with the principle that "what we look at determines our direction"? If so, how has this statement proven to be true in your life? What, then, should we purpose to do with our focus?

5. In this chapter, we read that waking up and looking up don't really help a person unless he takes the third, necessary step: He must rise up! When in your life did you have to do more than establish awareness and see another option? When did you have to take action? Are you naturally a decisive person who acts with conviction, or do you tend to be hesitant to act? Are there any specific actions that you need to take in your life right now to move forward and upward?

6. Think back through the teaching in this chapter about waking up, looking up, and rising up. List one thing you learned and one thing you can do right now that will allow you to begin accessing more of God's resurrection power—his *lift*—in your life.

CHAPTER THIRTEEN

Responding to Challenges: Daring To Turn Difficulty into Opportunity

"Opportunities energize the faithful and paralyze the fearful."
—Warren Wiersbe

A challenge can be perceived as a threat or as an opportunity. The way we respond to the challenge will significantly affect whether we shrink back in fear or spring forward in faith. Fear tries to turn opportunities into threats, whereas faith turns threats into opportunities. When Goliath cursed David and said, "Come over here, and I'll give your flesh to the birds and wild animals!" (1 Sam. 17:44, *NLT*), Goliath was certainly threatening David in every sense of the word. However, David chose to interpret the threat as an opportunity to demonstrate the faithfulness and greatness of God. To say that David rose to the challenge is a bit of an understatement. Not only did strong words of faith come out of David's mouth like a mighty torrent (1 Sam. 17:45-47), but his attitude translated into action: "So it was, when the Philistine arose and came and drew near to meet David, that David hurried and ran toward the army to meet the Philistine" (1 Sam. 17:48).

Admiral William Halsey once said, "There are no great people in this world, only great challenges which ordinary people rise to meet." Challenges aren't always negative and may not always come to us from an enemy. Challenges can be positive and issued from leaders, bosses, friends—people who hope to inspire us to action. Still, we have to choose what our attitude will be and how we will respond to the challenge in front of us.

Many of the extraordinary achievements and accomplishments in history happened as a response to challenges issued by inspiring leaders.

- Addressing the vastly outnumbered defenders of the Alamo, Colonel William Barrett Travis drew a line in the dirt with his sword and said, "I now want every man who is determined to stay here and die with me to come across this line."
- In Winston Churchill's first address as Prime Minister to the House of Commons, he spoke of the "ordeal of the most grievous kind" that was ahead of them, and said, "I have nothing to offer but blood, toil, tears, and sweat." Churchill's courage and fortitude set the mark to which the British people rose during World War II.
- In challenging the nation to put a man on the moon, President Kennedy said, "We choose to go to the moon in this decade… not because it is easy, but because it is hard, because that goal will serve to organize and measure the best of our energies and skills, because that challenge is one that we are willing to accept, one we are unwilling to postpone, and one which we intend to win."
- Martin Luther King Jr. challenged his country when he said, "I have a dream that one day this nation will rise up and live out

the true meaning of its creed: 'We hold these truths to be self-evident, that all men are created equal.'"

- Joshua challenged Israel when he said, "Choose for yourselves this day whom you will serve, whether the gods which your fathers served that were on the other side of the River, or the gods of the Amorites, in whose land you dwell. But as for me and my house, we will serve the Lord" (Josh. 24:15).

And what could have been a greater challenge than the one issued to us by the most inspiring leader of all, when Jesus says, "If anyone desires to come after Me, let him deny himself, and take up his cross daily, and follow Me" (Luke 9:23).

When some people think of challenges, they primarily think about spiritual attacks from the adversary or the multitude of problems in the world. God has called us to resist the enemy and to rise above the difficulties we face in life. These are challenges to which the believer shouts a defiant "No!" But there are other challenges that come to us in life, and those are the challenges that God gives us. These are not attacks that come to steal, kill, and destroy, but these are opportunities that push us to new limits, stretch us, move us from our comfort zone, and invite us to become more than we've ever been before. These are the challenges to which we must declare an emphatic "Yes!"

- Noah was challenged when God told him to build an ark.
- Abraham was challenged when God told him to leave his home country for an unknown destination.
- Jonah was challenged when God told him to go preach to the people of Nineveh in Assyria—Israel's great enemy.
- Mary was challenged when God told her that she as a virgin would bear a Son who would be the Savior of the world.
- Ananias was challenged when Jesus told him to go and pray for Saul of Tarsus, the greatest persecutor of the Church.

- Peter was challenged when God told him to go into the home of Cornelius and share the gospel with a group of Gentiles, something that was against his cultural upbringing.

All of these challenges resulted in obedience (for some, it was after initial reluctance) and in great blessing—for the one who answered the challenge and for many others affected by such obedience.

What are some of the challenges that God places before us today that we should respond to with obedience and action?

God Challenges Us To Go Places

Often, the places God challenges us to go to are places we never thought he would ask us to go. The first thing that might come to mind is missions work in foreign countries. However, most of us will never be asked by God to go to some remote part of the world. We should, though, be willing to go wherever God says to go and willing to help those who *are* called to go to distant lands with the gospel. Many people think only of the "big things" that God asks a small percentage of people to do, and in doing so they overlook the seemingly "small things" that God asks of each one of us. Where are some of the places God asks all of us to go?

- Go the extra mile (Matt. 5:41).
- Go and sin no more (John 8:11).
- Go and be reconciled to your brother (Matt. 5:24).
- Go in peace (Luke 7:50; 8:48).
- Go home (Matt. 9:6; Mark 5:19).

Let's talk for a moment about this last challenge: "Go home." Jesus made this same statement to a paralytic and a demoniac who had both been healed. While Jesus told his chosen apostles to go to the uttermost parts of the earth; he told others to simply *go home*. Our relationship with

God shouldn't merely affect our life and work *in the world*; it should also profoundly affect who we are behind closed doors and who we are around those closest to us. Abraham Lincoln said, "I care not for a man's religion whose dog and cat are not better off for it."

God Challenges Us To Give

Whenever the subject of "giving" comes up, most people automatically assume the conversation is going to be about money. The point here is not about money, but about the totality of our lives. In reality, God only wants two things from us—everything we are and everything we have. Once we have truly given these to him, everything else is easy.

General William Booth, founder of the Salvation Army, was asked the secret of his amazing Christian life. Booth answered, "I told the Lord that he could have all that there is of William Booth." That is the kind of consecration Jesus desires. In Luke 14:33, he states, "Any of you who does not give up everything he has cannot be my disciple."

Whatever giving we do in life—financial and otherwise—should flow from a heart and life that is first given to the Lord. This principle is exactly what Paul teaches in Second Corinthians, when he writes, "They first gave themselves to the Lord, and then to us by the will of God" (2 Cor. 8:5).

God Challenges Us To Grow

The principle of *growing* builds upon the first two principles of *going* and *giving*. When we go to the places God wants us to go, and when we give in the ways God wants us to give, we end up growing in the ways God wants us to grow.

Job is a tremendous example of someone who grew in ways he never thought he would have to grow. After all the horrific devastation Job faced in his life, God asked him to pray for the three men who had spoken so harshly and judgmentally against him. Job 42:10 states, "And the Lord restored Job's losses when he prayed for his friends. Indeed the Lord gave Job twice as much as he had before." Some have focused on the fact that Job got his stuff back, but his financial growth wasn't the greatest miracle. The real miracle was that his heart grew. Job overcame incredible anger and was able to pray for his friends. That is growth!

In chapter seven, we studied Gideon as the man who led Israel in overcoming the Midianites. But before Gideon could *go*, he had to *grow*. The angel had said to him, "*Go* in this might of yours" (Judges 6:14, emphasis mine), but before the going, Gideon had to grow. It was important that he overcome his fears, doubts, and sense of inferiority. If you go without growing first, you'll fail when you get there. If you give without growing first, your giving might be in vain. Paul tells us in First Corinthians 13:3, "And though I bestow all my goods to feed the poor, and though I give my body to be burned, but have not love, it profits me nothing."

God does not just want us going and giving; he wants us growing. God challenges us to go places we never thought he would ask us to go, to give in ways we never thought he would ask us to give, and to grow in ways we never thought he would ask us to grow. The only way for us to find genuine fulfillment in our journey is to obey God wholeheartedly in these areas.

Turning a *Challenge* into a *Cause*

I know that some believers are "on fire," or passionate about their walk with God, but I recently asked the Lord, "What will it take for Christians to awaken from their lethargy and complacency, to shake free from their preoccupation with self and become consumed with a passionate and compelling purpose—the purpose for which they were born?" In contemplating this, I have been reminded of the sacred fire that burned in the hearts of various spiritual leaders throughout history. Individuals who were aflame with a divine calling and destiny radically affected the course of human events. May we have such holy awakenings again! We live in a time when "going through the motions" and "business as usual" will not produce the results we need.

Turning again to the story of David and Goliath, we read that "a champion went out from the camp of the Philistines, named Goliath" (1 Sam. 17:4). Hell has always had its champions (and we see spiritual wickedness raising its ugly head in our day as well). While others cowered in fear, David arose in confidence, asking, "What shall be done for the man who kills this Philistine and takes away the reproach from Israel? For who is this uncircumcised Philistine, that he should defy the armies of the living God?" (1 Sam. 17:26). When his brothers criticized him for his proactive faith, accusing him of pride and insolence, David responded, "What have I done now? *Is there not a cause*?" (1 Sam. 17:29, emphasis mine). Because the Hebrew phrase that reads "is there not a cause" in the *New King James Version* is literally translated as "is it not a word," some commentators suggest that David simply wondered by his brothers were so mad at him for only asking a question. However, it seems obvious that David was in fact fighting for *a cause*—for a significant purpose—and that God's plan for him had radically empowered him to act. David had it in his heart that he was going to be the one to kill Goliath, and this resolve was a result of his faith in God.

Jeremiah Rose to the Challenge

The Old Testament prophet Jeremiah is another great leader who rose to a challenge and was motivated by a great cause. So great was his burden for Judah that Jeremiah was called "the Weeping Prophet." He prophesied during the years leading up to the Babylonian conquest of Jerusalem. Heavily persecuted, Jeremiah proclaims, "But if I say I'll never mention the Lord or speak in his name, his word burns in my heart like a fire. It's like a fire in my bones! I am worn out trying to hold it in! I can't do it!" (Jer. 20:9, *NLT*). Preachers should not step into the pulpit because they *have to say something*, but because they *have something to say*. Jeremiah spoke words from the heart and mind of God—the words were "live coals off the altar" and seared the souls of his listeners. Jeremiah was compelled to tell the people of Israel the unpleasant truth that because of their persistent rebellion, they would endure Babylonian captivity for seventy years until God ultimately delivered them. While the false prophets said that everything was going to be okay, Jeremiah's cause made him unpopular with people but lifted him into greatness in the eyes of God.

The Apostles Responded to Challenges

When Peter and John were threatened and told not to speak anymore in the name of Jesus, they responded, "We cannot but speak the things which we have seen and heard" (Acts 4:20). Where did such boldness come from? This world had not lulled them into complacency. They were not preoccupied with anything this world had to offer. A.W. Tozer, famed American preacher and author, writes:

> The Early Church was in wonderment at Christ. He dazzled them and stirred within such feelings of amazement that they

> could never get over Christ. All they talked about was Christ. All they thought about, from morning to night, was Christ. Christ was their only reason for living, and they were more than willing to die for Him.[27]

It is much easier to respond positively to a threat and rise to a difficult challenge when a great cause is burning in your heart! That is exactly what the Early Church did, and they did it time and time again.

Paul (Formerly Known as Saul)

Before his conversion, Saul of Tarsus was tenacious in his determination to destroy Christians. When he was transformed by his encounter with Jesus, those destructive desires were replaced by holy ambition and sanctified resolve. There was nothing casual or lax about his commitment. Paul was 100% in! We clearly see his consecration in the way he spoke about those in his culture who did not know Jesus. He writes:

ROMANS 9:1-3 (*NLT*)
1 With Christ as my witness, I speak with utter truthfulness. My conscience and the Holy Spirit confirm it.

2 My heart is filled with bitter sorrow and unending grief

3 for my people, my Jewish brothers and sisters. I would be willing to be forever cursed—cut off from Christ! —if that would save them.

We seldom hear such words today. How many people are satisfied as long as they and their loved ones are saved? Who is crying out for the lost? Paul was moved by a great cause—God's love for lost humanity! He persisted in ministry because threats and challenges were eclipsed by what

[27] A. W. Tozer, *The Dangers of a Shallow Faith: Awakening from Spiritual Lethargy* (Ventura, CA: Gospel Light, 2012), 32.

he saw as an opportunity to reach people with the gospel. Tozer—who I quoted previously—describes this kind of dedication:

> Come near to the holy men and women of the past and you will soon feel the heat of their desire after God. They mourned for Him, they prayed and wrestled and sought for Him day and night, in season and out, and when they found Him, the finding was all the sweeter for the long seeking.[28]

We need a host of believers and ministers today who possess the same passionate commitment that Paul demonstrated and that Tozer described.

Martin Luther King Jr.'s Dream

Dr. Martin Luther King Jr., the great civil rights leader, once said, "Even if they try to kill you, you develop the inner conviction that there are some things so precious, some things so eternally true that they are worth dying for. And if a person has not found something to die for, that person isn't fit to live!" Martin Luther King Jr. was "all in." He drew a line in the sand of society, and then boldly stepped over it. A consuming, burning vision governed him, guided him, and compelled him to move forward in the face of horrific opposition. The man who said, "I have a dream," truly did have a dream—an all-consuming vision—and his efforts and energies toward fulfilling that dream changed a nation.

It is important to note that the motivation inside the people we've studied in this chapter was not madness or hype or a matter of overwrought emotions. The bold declarations of duty and consecration in response to the challenges they faced certainly contain emotional elements, but evangelist F.B. Meyer had it right when he said, "Consecration is not the act

[28] A. W. Tozer, *The Pursuit of God* (Christian Miracle Foundation Press, 2011), loc. 154, Kindle.

of our feelings but of our will." If we are to experience the resurrected—or *lifted*—life, we must be willing to view challenges as opportunities and this kind of perspective will require us to consecrate ourselves.

Perhaps this is a good time for many of us to take inventory of ourselves and ask some hard questions:

- Do we passionately love Jesus and others the way we used to (see Rev. 2:4), or have we somehow regressed and reverted to just "going through the motions"?
- Do we need—with the help of the Holy Spirit—to eradicate complacency, lethargy, religious boredom, or apathy from our lives?
- Are we preoccupied with earthly, temporal things—just "hanging out" spiritually and looking forward to heaven when we die?
- Have we become numb and de-sensitized to vital and essential spiritual things because of the pressures of the world?
- Do we have a yearning, burning, compelling, passionate desire to see the lost saved, the saved discipled, the Church thriving, and the plan of God fulfilled in the earth?

Let us do what Paul admonishes Timothy: "Stir up (rekindle the embers of, fan the flame of, and keep burning) the [gracious] gift of God, [the inner fire] that is in you..." (2 Tim. 2:6, *AMP*). This is a strong admonishment, but it parallels what Jesus tells the Church in Sardis:

REVELATION 3:2 (*AMP*)
2 Rouse yourselves and keep awake, and strengthen and invigorate what remains and is on the point of dying; for I have not found a thing that you have done [any work of yours] meeting the requirements of My God or perfect in His sight.

The Message renders the next verse, "Think of the gift you once had in your hands, the Message you heard with your ears—grasp it again and turn back to God."

I am excited about the future, and I see great days ahead for the Church. It is time for us to experience what Andrew Murray describes: "A true revival means nothing less than a revolution, casting out the spirit of worldliness and selfishness, and making God and his love triumph in the heart and life." Likewise, Leonard Ravenhill remarks, "As long as we are content to live without revival, we will." My prayer is that a great host of today's believers will rise to the fullness of our calling and respond to God's desire to fully express himself in the earth.

❗ A Resurrection Declaration

Lord, I ask you to help me see opportunities in the challenges I face and to help me be energized by them. I want to respond in faith to every situation that I encounter in life. Help me have an optimistic, can-do attitude about all that I face, and to keep in mind that it is through your strength and ability that I can prevail. Like Paul, I say, "I can do all things through Christ who strengthens me." I consecrate myself to go wherever you want me to go, whether it is a geographical location or simply to a place of greater spiritual maturity and development. I commit to giving in all the ways you desire me to give, and I start by giving myself entirely to you. Beyond that, all that I have is yours as well. Finally, I dedicate myself to growing in all the ways you desire that I grow. I believe you are helping me—by your Word and by your Spirit—to become all that you've asked me to become. As you've helped so many of your servants through the ages, help me turn a challenge into a cause, and let me live with a sense of divine purpose for your glory and honor. In Jesus' name, I pray—amen.

Bonus Quotes

"There are no great people in this world, only great challenges which ordinary people rise to meet."

—William Frederick Halsey, Jr.

"Man's extremity is God's opportunity."

—John Flavel

"Oh, when shall we learn how unspeakably pleasing obedience is in God's sight, and how unspeakable is the reward He bestows upon it."

—Andrew Murray

"When God gave Christ to this world, He gave the best He had, and He wants us to do the same."

—D.L. Moody

"Growth is the only evidence of life."

—John Henry Newman

Lyrics that Lift: Hymns of the Resurrection

From "Blest Morning, Whose Young Dawning Rays" by Isaac Watts (1709)

Hell and the grave unite their force

To hold our God in vain;

The sleeping Conqueror arose,

And burst their feeble chain.

Questions for Reflection and Discussion

1. Do you tend to see challenges as threats or opportunities? Have there been situations in which you've been paralyzed by fear instead of energized by faith?

2. Even though the challenge might not seem daunting to others, have you been challenged in such a way that required you to really trust God? Have there been challenges that you would not have been able to face without God's strength?

3. Are there places where God has challenged you to go? Were these geographical places, or were these some of the "spiritual places" described in this chapter (e.g., go the extra mile, go and be reconciled to your brother, and so forth)? How did you respond to the challenge, and what was the outcome?

4. Has God ever challenged you by asking you to give something you were reluctant to give? Was this a financial gift or something else? Did God challenge you to give up a habit or to surrender some aspect of your life to him? What was your initial reaction when you felt God's leading? Was it a struggle to give? What was the outcome when you obeyed?

5. Have you grown in ways that you never thought you'd be asked to grow? What elements contributed to your spiritual growth and the growth of your character? In what ways has growth been joyful, and in what ways has it been painful? Are you aware of additional areas in your life where growth is still needed? Do you have a plan to help you grow in these areas?

6. Think back through the teaching in this chapter about how to turn difficult challenges into opportunities. List one thing you learned and one thing you can do right now that will allow you to begin accessing more of God's resurrection power—his *lift*—in your life.

CHAPTER FOURTEEN

Creating a Culture of Constant Improvement

"There's a better way to do it. Find it!"
—Thomas A. Edison

As I travel to churches year after year, I am continually amazed by the various combinations of strengths and weaknesses in different congregations. No congregation is perfect, and every church has both strengths that are commendable as well as areas that can be improved. Churches in the New Testament era were no different. In my opinion, the way Jesus addressed the various congregations in Asia Minor (in Revelation chapters 2 and 3) is one of the most fascinating biblical studies.

One of the congregations I find especially interesting is the Church at Thyatira. Most who have a cursory knowledge of Jesus' admonitions in this section of Scripture will immediately identify this church with Jezebel, a leader who grievously taught a terribly misleading doctrine of compromise.

This corrupt teaching facilitated and encouraged immorality and idolatry among the believers in Thyatira—behaviors that Jesus hated. As heinous as these behaviors were, Jesus still saw good in this congregation, recognizing that not everyone was participating in the poisonous error. Rather, some believers had maintained a kind of immunity to Jezebel's teaching and were actually doing quite well.

Jesus gives a glowing commendation to this church when he states, "I know your works, love, service, faith, and your patience; and as for your works, the last are more than the first" (Rev. 2:19).

Based on this statement, we understand that many of the believers in this congregation were experiencing growth, maturity, and productivity in spite of corruption elsewhere within the church. These godly members had a lot going for them, and they were increasing in fruitfulness. Their latter works, Jesus states, were greater than their early works. Consider how Revelation 2:19 reads in three other translations (emphasis mine):

- "I see everything you're doing for me. Impressive! The love and the faith, the service and persistence. Yes, very impressive! *You get better at it every day*" (*MSG*).
- "I know all the things you do. I have seen your love, your faith, your service, and your patient endurance. And I can see *your constant improvement* in all these things" (*NLT*).
- "I know your deeds, your love and faith, your service and perseverance, and that *you are now doing more than you did at first*" (*NIV*).

Yes, the Thyatiran Church had a cancer in it, but it had not metastasized throughout the whole body. Jesus made it clear that if repentance did not occur, he would deal swiftly and severely with those involved (Rev. 2:21-23). Fortunately, though, there was still some health in the church, and in a very real sense, some believers were doing tremendously well.

Every church would consider it a great honor for Jesus to commend their constant improvement and increased accomplishments in such vital areas as he commended those in Thyatira.

One of the sad things I often hear while traveling pertains to believers who are not exhibiting the positive trait of the Thyatiran believers. They are not demonstrating constant improvement and are not getting better at serving God, even though they have received healthy biblical teaching. I often hear from pastors concerning key individuals who have served God vigorously and fervently in the past but are now deciding that it is all right for them to enter into some kind of "spiritual retirement" when it comes to volunteering and working in the ministry of helps. This trend reminds me a bit about what was happening in another New Testament Church—the Church in Ephesus.

Before I expound on a current trend in churches today, let me present a simple contrast between the Church at Thyatira and the Church at Ephesus.

- The Church in Thyatira had a corrupt (and corrupting) individual in leadership who advocated very bad doctrine. However, several in the church were walking in great love and growing in their productivity and good works. They were doing more for God than they had previously.
- The Church in Ephesus' leadership was very dedicated to accurate doctrine, but there had been a radical decline in the amount of love being exhibited and good works being done. These believers were doing less for God than they had previously.

These two congregations had polar opposite strengths and weaknesses!

After commending the Ephesian believers for their tenacious commitment to doctrinal purity, Jesus remarks:

REVELATION 2:4-5 (*NLT*)

4 But I have this complaint against you. You don't love me or each other as you did at first!

5 Look how far you have fallen! Turn back to me and do the works you did at first. If you don't repent, I will come and remove your lampstand from its place among the churches.

The Church in Ephesus had correct doctrine, but they had completely collapsed in the area of love and in carrying out the good works that love produces. As a general rule, right doctrine *tends* to produce right behavior, and as a general rule, wrong doctrine *tends* to produce wrong behavior, but in this case, there was an unusual reversal of the norm.

We learn from these Churches that Jesus is pleased to commend Christians wherever they are doing well, but he insists that we correct what is wrong. He was not willing to tolerate morally corrupting doctrine, and he was not willing to tolerate a lack of love and laziness. He told both groups to repent!

As a teacher, I have always been very focused on having right doctrine, and I believe this is still vitally important. It is a major emphasis of the New Testament. However, there is a great need for believers to have more than just a correct set of beliefs to which they give mental assent. Churches today are in need of believers who passionately love Jesus and who are doing the "first works"—working with the same fervency and enthusiasm as when they were first saved. Christians do not need to choose between having right doctrine (beliefs) and right behavior (works); we should earnestly pursue both!

When it comes to the common complaint I hear from today's pastors, I understand that people may retire from certain jobs or careers, but I don't see anywhere in the Bible where people are encouraged to quit serving

Jesus and sit back and let someone else be responsible for serving God. If we have physical limitations, we can certainly pray, and praying is certainly not the least expression of serving. I even understand that a pastor might step aside from carrying the specific load of the pastoral *office*, but we are still called to love and serve God even if we don't stand in a particular office. Consider these passages:

PSALM 92:13-14 (*NKJV*)
13 Those who are planted in the house of the Lord shall flourish in the courts of our God.

14 They shall still bear fruit in old age; they shall be fresh and flourishing.

DEUTERONOMY 33:25 (*NKJV*)
25 As your days, so shall your strength be.

25 May you have lifelong strength (*NET*).

25 May... your strength last as long as you live (*HCSB*).

I love what an 85-year-old Caleb tells Joshua:

JOSHUA 14:10-12 (*NET*)
10 the Lord has preserved my life, just as he promised, these past forty-five years since the Lord spoke these words to Moses, during which Israel traveled through the wilderness. Now look, I am today eighty-five years old.

11 Today I am still as strong as when Moses sent me out. I can fight and go about my daily activities with the same energy I had then.

12 Now, assign me this hill country which the Lord promised me at that time! ...assuming the Lord is with me, I will conquer them, as the Lord promised."

We will never reach a time when we have the right to stop fulfilling God's plan for our life. No matter our age, we have no expiration date!

May we be committed to experiencing the best of all that God charges—and enables us—to have! May we receive good, strong, healthy, solid doctrine, and may we be full of fervent love and abounding in good works for Jesus! May we continually allow God to lift us to where he wants us to be, as he moves us from ordinary to extraordinary and from natural to supernatural.

! A Resurrection Declaration

Lord, I recognize today that I am a work in progress, and I also believe that you, who began a good work in me, will perform it until the day of Christ Jesus. I desire that my latter works be greater than my earlier works, and I desire that my love for you and others will never wane but will grow stronger throughout my life here on earth. I pray that my life will be marked by an attitude of constant improvement, that I will not grow apathetic, complacent, or lethargic. I desire to always manifest high quality and excellence so that you may be glorified. Even into my old age, I desire to bear fruit and be fresh and flourishing. In Jesus' name, I pray—amen.

Bonus Quotes

"When you do the common things in life in an uncommon way, you will command the attention of the world."

—George Washington Carver

"And when you discover what you will be in your life, set out to do it as if God Almighty called you at this particular moment in history to do it. Don't just set out to do a good job."

—Martin Luther King, Jr.

"In the race for quality, there is no finish line."

—David T. Kearns

"We all want progress, but if you're on the wrong road, progress means doing an about-turn and walking back to the right road; in that case, the man who turns back soonest is the most progressive."

—C.S. Lewis

"If you be faithful, you will have that honor that comes from God: his Spirit will say in your hearts, 'Well done, good and faithful servants.'"

—Adam Clarke

 Lyrics that Lift: Hymns of the Resurrection

From "Arise, My Soul, Awake and Sing" by Arthur T. Russell (1851)

Arise, my soul, awake and sing
The triumphs of thy heavenly king;
The Lord is risen, His foes are fled;
He reigns the Lord of quick and dead.

So shall His saints with gladness rise
And rest on Him their joyful eyes;
Then shall they mourn and weep no more,
But with eternal praise adore.

 Questions for Reflection and Discussion

1. Consider Thomas Edison's statement: "There's a better way to do it. Find it!" Do you like this statement, or do you find it unsettling? Are you a person who tends to repeat previous behaviors, or do you seek innovation and improvement?
2. Considering the believers in Thyatira, would you say that your good works for the Lord have increased over time? Are you getting better at them and experiencing constant improvement?
3. Considering the believers in Ephesus, have you maintained your first love? Do you still passionately love Jesus and others? Are you still working for God as you once did, or do you need to (as Jesus admonished the Ephesians), "Turn back to [him] and do the works you did at first" (Rev. 2:5, *NLT*)?
4. Jesus not only corrected the New Testament believers where adjustments were necessary, but he also commended them in areas where they were doing well. Some believers seem to think that Jesus will only do one or the other. Have there been times when you have sensed the Lord's affirmation over your life? Have there been times when you've felt the Lord directing you to make adjustments? Do you have an open ear to hear both types of communication from the Lord?
5. Do you envision a time when you will "retire" from your work for Jesus, or do you believe that you will serve him until you leave this earth?
6. Think back through the teaching in this chapter about constant improvement. List one thing you learned and one thing you can do right now that will allow you to begin accessing more of God's resurrection power—his *lift*—in your life.

CHAPTER FIFTEEN

Our God Is the God of Increase

He will love you,
He will bless you,
He will increase you.
—Deuteronomy 7:13(*MSG*)

What do you think of when you hear the phrase "the God of Increase?" Do you think of God helping you *have* more, or do you see him helping you *become* more and *achieve* more? God is vitally interested in developing *you* as a person—enabling you to become everything he wants you to be and empowering you to accomplish the things he wants you to accomplish. Consider Paul's powerful admonition to the Corinthian Church:

2 CORINTHIANS 6:11-13 (*MSG*)
11 I can't tell you how much I long for you to enter this wide-open, spacious life.

12 We don't fence you in. The smallness you feel comes from within you. Your lives aren't small, but you're living them in a small way.

13 I'm speaking as plainly as I can with great affection. Open up your lives. Live openly and expansively!

Something had been happening in the hearts and minds of these believers to restrict and constrict their relationship not only with Paul but also with God. As a result, they were living below the vast grandeur and expanding goodness that God intended for them. Paul wanted them to realize the full potential of everything God had made available to them.

It is important that we acknowledge and trust God as a God of Increase! We see continually that whatever God touches flourishes and increases. In his creative work, God did not make a dull, stagnant planet. Rather, earth is teeming with life—all by God's design. Everything he created was destined to grow, multiply, and increase. Even man was instructed to "be fruitful, and multiply, and replenish the earth, and subdue it: and have dominion…" (Gen. 1:28).

God's propensity to increase is evident in his dealings with Abraham. Consider what God communicates to him (Gen 12:2; 17:2, 6):

- I will make you a great nation.
- I will bless you.
- I will make your name great.
- You shall be a blessing.
- I will multiply you exceedingly.
- I will make you exceedingly fruitful.

We may not be called to do exactly what Abraham was called to do, but we serve the same God that Abraham served. God spoke with Abraham at different times about increase before the increase actually materialized, and Abraham believed what God said about increase before the increase took place.

Even Jesus experienced increase because of his relationship with the Heavenly Father. Luke writes that, "Jesus increased in wisdom and stature, and in favor with God and men" (Luke 2:52). John 10:10 gives great insight into Jesus' mission: "The thief does not come except to steal, and to kill, and to destroy. I have come that they may have life, and that they may have it more abundantly." Satan's work of stealing, killing, and destroying speaks of decrease. In clear contrast, Jesus' work of giving life and giving it more abundantly speaks of increase. Even in the Old Testament, Isaiah prophesied of increase that would occur due to Jesus' ever-expanding influence. The prophet writes, "Of the increase of his government and peace there will be no end" (Isa. 9:7).

It is very important that we not apply a worldly view of increase to God's work in our lives. If Christians take a shallow, carnal, and materialistic view of increase, they may think that their faith will create for them a smooth upward path to success without any hindrances or setbacks along the way. We cannot gauge ultimate increase by momentary circumstances. When Jesus was criticized, ridiculed, and rejected, God still had a plan of increase in place for him. When multitudes got offended and left Jesus, and even when his own disciples abandoned him, God still had an ultimate purpose of increase for Jesus. When he was arrested, falsely accused, beaten, and crucified, increase was still in Jesus' future. For Jesus, increase was manifested in his resurrection—and in the resulting harvest of our souls when we came into relationship with God because of him.

Jesus received the *product* of increase, but he was also willing to go through the *process* that ultimately brought him that increase. The lesson here for us is very important. People sometimes have to be willing to pay a price to get the right results. At certain stages, it might appear that we're going backward or downward, but these steps are often a vital part of the journey that ultimately leads onward and upward. This can require radical obedience and absolute trust—the kind of obedience that Jesus exhibited:

PHILIPPIANS 2:7-9

7 [Jesus] made himself of no reputation, taking the form of a bondservant, and coming in the likeness of men.

8 And being found in appearance as a man, he humbled himself and became obedient to the point of death, even the death of the cross.

9 Therefore God also has highly exalted him and given him the name which is above every name....

We don't necessarily experience increase by grabbing for the best and the highest. Sometimes we achieve true elevation by humbling ourselves and simply doing things God's way. For example, Jesus states, "Unless a grain of wheat falls into the ground and dies, it remains alone; but if it dies, it produces much grain" (John 12:24). True productivity, growth, and increase—according to Jesus—can occur *ultimately* even when there is an appearance of loss *initially.*

This paradoxical principle is illustrated by John the Baptist concerning his role and relationship with Jesus when he states, "[Jesus] must increase, but I must decrease" (John 3:30). John lived for the increase of Jesus, not for his own self-promotion. He knew that he would serve the Kingdom of God best by taking a secondary, supportive role to Jesus rather than trying to advance himself or campaign for recognition and popularity. For John, true increase (or promotion) came from embracing less exposure for himself and investing his energies into promoting Jesus. Initially, John's actions seemed like a step down, but ultimately his decision earned words of honor: Jesus says, "Among those born of women there is not a greater prophet than John the Baptist" (Luke 7:28). Understanding this principle can help prevent us from walking in a fleshly, carnal, get-to-the-top-at-any-cost type of ambition that is superficial and can cost us our integrity.

There remains a godly increase that we should acknowledge, embrace, and celebrate. Let us look at five specific areas where God wants us to experience this kind of increase.

1. God wants us to increase in our knowledge of him.

God wants us to know *him*, not just know *about* him. And God desires that our knowledge of him grow, increase, and develop over time. Scripture makes this abundantly clear.

JEREMIAH 9:23-24

23 Thus says the Lord: "Let not the wise man glory in his wisdom, let not the mighty man glory in his might, nor let the rich man glory in his riches;

24 But let him who glories glory in this, that he understands and knows me, that I am the Lord, exercising lovingkindness, judgment, and righteousness in the earth. For in these I delight," says the Lord.

JOHN 17:3

3 And this is eternal life, that they may know you, the only true God, and Jesus Christ whom You have sent.

PHILIPPIANS 3:10 (*AMP*)

10 [For my determined purpose is] that I may know him [that I may progressively become more deeply and intimately acquainted with him, perceiving and recognizing and understanding the wonders of his person more strongly and more clearly].

COLOSSIANS 1:9-10 (*NLT*)

9 We ask God to give you complete knowledge of his will and to give you spiritual wisdom and understanding.

10 Then the way you live will always honor and please the Lord, and your lives will produce every kind of good fruit. All the while, you will grow as you learn to know God better and better.

2 PETER 1:2 (*NET*)

2 May grace and peace be lavished on you as you grow in the rich knowledge of God and of Jesus our Lord!

Not only can we know God, we can know him better and better as time goes on—the more we study the Bible and the more we walk with him.

I am amazed sometimes when I hear people say that we can't really know God because he is mysterious and beyond our comprehension. There is certainly an element of mystery concerning the things of God, and none of us knows everything, but God in his goodness has chosen to reveal and make himself known to us. If God really did not want us to know him, he would not have inspired the writing of Scripture, nor would he have sent Jesus or the Holy Spirit to the earth. He could have left us totally in the dark, but he chose not to do that. Concerning the things of God, Paul writes:

1 CORINTHIANS 2:10-12 (*NLT*)

10 It was to us that God revealed these things by his Spirit. For his Spirit searches out everything and shows us God's deep secrets.

11 No one can know a person's thoughts except that person's own spirit, and no one can know God's thoughts except God's own Spirit.

12 And we have received God's Spirit (not the world's spirit), so we can know the wonderful things God has freely given us.

God absolutely wants us to know him, and although we will not know everything about him until we get to heaven (1 Cor. 13:9-12), we can still continually increase in the knowledge of him during our time here on earth.

2. God wants us to increase in godliness.

Jesus spoke of an increase in lawlessness in the last days (Matt. 24:12), and Paul also describes increasing ungodliness in the last days in Second Timothy 3:1-12, and then states, "But evil men and impostors will grow worse and worse, deceiving and being deceived" (2 Tim. 3:13). Paul also advises Timothy to "shun profane and idle babblings, for they will increase to more ungodliness" (2 Tim. 2:16). If ungodliness can increase, it only seems logical that godliness can increase as well, and Scripture supports this idea.

In Second Peter 1:5-7, the apostle teaches that we can add various characteristics to our faith. One of these is godliness (along with virtue, self-control, brotherly kindness, and so forth). He then states, "For if these qualities are yours and are increasing, they keep you from being ineffective or unfruitful in the knowledge of our Lord Jesus Christ" (2 Pet. 1:8). Clearly, godliness—along with the other traits—are characteristics in which the Christian can increase.

As believers, we have the privilege and the responsibility of growing in the things of God. This includes godliness, holiness, and sanctification. God makes us righteous (in that he puts us in right standing with himself) when we are born again, and then we get to grow in all things pertaining to God and his plan for our life. Whether it is the admonition in Hebrews

12:1 to "lay aside every weight, and the sin which so easily ensnares us" or Paul's encouragement to Timothy to cleanse himself from dishonorable and corrupting behavior (2 Tim. 2:21), it is clear that the follower of Christ is called to increase in godliness throughout his spiritual journey.

3. God wants us to increase in love toward one another.

Other than the reality of God's love for us, there is perhaps nothing more clearly and powerfully communicated in Scripture than God's desire (actually his commandment) for us to love him and to love one another (Matt. 22:36-40; John 13:34-35). Paul expresses his heartfelt desire for churches in the New Testament in these passages:

PHILIPPIANS 1:9 (*NLT*)
9 I pray that your love will overflow more and more, and that you will keep on growing in knowledge and understanding.

1 THESSALONIANS 3:12 (*AMP*)
12 And may the Lord make you to increase and excel and overflow in love for one another and for all people, just as we also do for you.

1 THESSALONIANS 4:9-10
9 But concerning brotherly love you have no need that I should write to you, for you yourselves are taught by God to love one another;

10 and indeed you do so toward all the brethren who are in all Macedonia. But we urge you, brethren, that you increase more and more.

It is by our mutual love that we comfort, encourage, and edify one another, and as Jesus states, it is our *love for one another* that will prove to the world that we are his disciples (John 13:35).

4. God wants us to increase in strength and power.

In the world, the strong often rule over the weak. In God's Kingdom, the principles that govern the proper use of strength and power are radically different. Strength is not given so that we can strut around like a rooster or peacock, vainly drawing attention to ourselves. Strength is a gift from God that enables us to help others, not to dominate or exploit them. Romans 15:1 in *The Message* reads, "Those of us who are strong and able in the faith need to step in and lend a hand to those who falter, and not just do what is most convenient for us. Strength is for service, not status."

While it is true that power often corrupts people, causing them to forget God and bringing out the worst in them, it does not have to be this way. If we stay humble before God and wisely use whatever he gives us for his glory, God can trust us with much. It is important, though, that we are diligent to keep a proper perspective of power and strength. We are not to come to God *in* our strength; we are to come to God *for* our strength. Scripture is full of examples of people who acknowledged their need for and dependence upon God. All went well for them as long as they remembered that God was their source and that the strength they received was for his glory.

Paul is a great example of this. When Paul was troubled over a messenger of Satan (which he called "a thorn in the flesh"), he cried out to God for help. What was the Lord's response?

> **2 CORINTHIANS 12:9**
> **9 He said to me, "My grace is sufficient for you, for my strength is made perfect in weakness." Therefore most gladly I will rather boast in my infirmities, that the power of Christ may rest upon me.**

Paul had come to the end of himself, and there he found strength from God.

Paul's situation was not unlike that of some of the heroes of faith described in the Old Testament. Scripture states, "Their weakness was turned to strength. They became strong in battle and put whole armies to flight" (Heb. 11:34, *NLT*). I really appreciate the way one translation renders this: "From being weaklings they became strong men and mighty warriors." Christians need not fear that God will condemn us or look down on us because of our weaknesses. On the contrary, Jesus empathizes with us and offers us comfort and support. The Bible tells us that Jesus "understands our weaknesses, for he faced all of the same testings we do, yet he did not sin" (Heb. 4:15, *NLT*).

We should keep in mind that God's power and resurrection are inextricably linked. Romans 1:4 proclaims that Jesus was "declared to be the Son of God with power according to the Spirit of holiness, by the resurrection from the dead. Likewise, Paul also teaches that, "God both raised up the Lord and will also raise us up by His power" (1 Cor. 16:4). Another very meaningful verse contrasts weakness and power as they relate to the crucifixion and the resurrection.

2 CORINTHIANS 13:4
4 For though he was crucified in weakness, yet he lives by the power of God. For we also are weak in him, but we shall live with him by the power of God toward you.

It may seem paradoxical when we consider the power-weakness relationship in Scripture, but remember that God is the One who will ultimately reconcile all things and make all things right. Those who arrogantly flaunt power in a godless way will someday find themselves brought to nothing. However, those who humble themselves before God and acknowledge their profound need for him will find themselves strengthened tremendously.

A few other scriptures reveal God's desire to strengthen us in this life:

PSALM 75:10 (*NLT*)
10 For God says, "I will break the strength of the wicked, but I will increase the power of the godly."

PROVERBS 24:5
5 A wise man is strong, yes, a man of knowledge increases strength.

ISAIAH 40:29-31 (*NLT*)
29 He gives power to the weak and strength to the powerless.

30 Even youths will become weak and tired, and young men will fall in exhaustion.

31 But those who trust in the Lord will find new strength. They will soar high on wings like eagles. They will run and not grow weary. They will walk and not faint.

EPHESIANS 6:10
10 Be strong in the Lord and in the power of His might.

2 TIMOTHY 2:1

1 Be strong in the grace that is in Christ Jesus.

God has made his strength available to us, and he has made known his intentions regarding our partaking of his strength. In Philippians 3:10, Paul expresses his desire to know Christ more intimately, but also to "come to know the power outflowing from His resurrection [which it exerts over believers]" (*AMP*). What an amazing thought! The power that flows out from the resurrection of Christ exerts its influence over believers. What a great source of empowerment for each of us!

Why does God want to empower us, and why does he want us to be strong in him?

- So that we can glorify Him.
- So that we can live godly lives in this world.
- So that we can help others who need help.
- So that we can live victoriously in this life.
- So that we can be effective witnesses.
- So that we can be godly people (husbands, wives, parents, employees, friends, and so forth).

5. God wants us to increase in resources and generosity.

There are many warnings in Scripture against greed and covetousness and against the pitfalls of trusting in money. However, it is also true that God created this earth to yield its provisions for the benefit of the people he created and loves. While the Bible's core message is certainly not a get-rich-quick scheme, its principles, when properly applied, typically lead people into greater prosperity in their lives. It is difficult to read through the Book of Proverbs without recognizing multiple passages that teach us how to advance and do better in life. I'm not talking about the dubious claims of "Give Preacher So-and-So $1,000 and expect your miracle harvest." I'm speaking of the biblical principles of fearing God, shunning evil, walking in integrity, working hard, and being generous. On a practical level, every pastor and missionary can tell you that it is extremely helpful in carrying out God's work if there are generous people who have ample provision from which they can give. Even Jesus benefitted from the regular financial support of generous people. At one point in Jesus' ministry we read:

LUKE 8:1-3 (*NLT*)

1 He took his twelve disciples with him,

2 along with some women who had been cured of evil spirits and diseases. Among them were Mary Magdalene, from whom he had cast out seven demons;

3 Joanna, the wife of Chuza, Herod's business manager; Susanna; and many others who were contributing from their own resources to support Jesus and his disciples.

Jesus loves everyone—rich and poor alike—and his love is not based on a person's bank account. Even so, there were some people of means who used their resources to support his work.

God's Word is full of admonitions that will help us prosper and do well in life. Just as Scripture provides numerous words of instruction on how to increase in other areas of life, the Bible also says much about our increasing in financial and material areas.

PROVERBS 10:22

22 The blessing of the Lord makes one rich, and he adds no sorrow with it.

PROVERBS 11:24 (*MSG*)

24 The world of the generous gets larger and larger; the world of the stingy gets smaller and smaller.

PROVERBS 11:25 (*NLT*)

25 The generous will prosper; those who refresh others will themselves be refreshed.

PROVERBS 13:4 (*NLT*)

4 Lazy people want much but get little, but those who work hard will prosper.

PROVERBS 16:20 (*NLT*)

20 Those who listen to instruction will prosper; those who trust the Lord will be joyful.

God's Word is also full of teaching about being generous givers to support the work of the gospel and to help others.

There are two churches in particular that Paul addresses about their giving—the Church in Corinth and the Church in Philippi. The following verses all pertain to the believers' finances and their attitudes and actions regarding generosity.

2 CORINTHIANS 8:7 (*NLT*)

7 Since you excel in so many ways—in your faith, your gifted speakers, your knowledge, your enthusiasm, and your love from us—I want you to excel also in this gracious act of giving.

2 CORINTHIANS 9:6-8

6 He who sows sparingly will also reap sparingly, and he who sows bountifully will also reap bountifully.

7 So let each one give as he purposes in his heart, not grudgingly or of necessity; for God loves a cheerful giver.

8 And God is able to make all grace abound toward you, that you, always having all sufficiency in all things, may have an abundance for every good work.

2 CORINTHIANS 9:10 (*NLT*)

10 For God is the one who provides seed for the farmer and then bread to eat. In the same way, he will provide and increase your resources and then produce a great harvest of generosity in you.

PHILIPPIANS 4:18-19 (*NLT*)

18 I am generously supplied with the gifts you sent me with Epaphroditus. They are a sweet-smelling sacrifice that is acceptable and pleasing to God.

19 And this same God who takes care of me will supply all your needs from his glorious riches, which have been given to us in Christ Jesus.

Many of the scriptures about increase and generosity in the Bible specifically refer to money. But keep in mind that generosity is about more than just finances. God can help us be generous with our time, our talents, our encouragement, and other resources.

God is happy to bless us just because we are his children. Jesus states, "Do not fear, little flock, for it is your Father's good pleasure to give you the kingdom" (Luke 12:32). In addition, God is also pleased to supply us richly in all things so that we can be a distributor of his blessings to others.

God is a God of increase! He desires that we increase in our knowledge of him, in godliness, in love toward one another, in strength and power, and in resources and generosity. He not only desires our increase, but he has also given us his Word and Spirit to make increase possible. As we experience this increase, let us always keep God first and promote his glory in every way. We have not been lifted for our own glory—but for God's.

❗ A Resurrection Declaration

Lord, I thank you that you are a God of increase and multiplication and that you have called me to a wide-open, spacious life. You are the God who made Abraham's name great; you multiplied him exceedingly; and you made him exceedingly fruitful. Abraham is the father of our faith, and I believe that you have great blessings and increase in store for me today. Help me to increase in every way that you desire. I believe that you want me to increase in the knowledge of you, in godliness, in love for others, in strength and power, and in resources and generosity. None of this increase is for the gratification of my ego, but for the glory of your Name and for the expansion of your influence in the earth. In Jesus' name, I pray—amen.

Bonus Quotes

"May God so fill us today with the heart of Christ that we may glow with the divine fire of holy desire."

—A. B. Simpson

"We can be tired, weary and emotionally distraught, but after spending time alone with God, we find that He injects into our bodies energy, power and strength."

—Charles Stanley

"When a man has no strength, if he leans on God, he becomes powerful."

—D. L. Moody

"The soul's deepest thirst is for God Himself, who has made us so that we can never be satisfied without Him."

—F. F. Bruce

"A baptism of holiness, a demonstration of godly living is the crying need of our day."

—Duncan Campbell

 Lyrics that Lift: Hymns of the Resurrection

From "I Know That My Redeemer Lives" by Samuel Medley (1775)

I know that my Redeemer lives!

What joy this blest assurance gives!

He lives, he lives, who once was dead;

He lives, my ever-living Head!

He lives triumphant from the grave;

He lives eternally to save;

He lives exalted, throned above;

He lives to rule his church in love.

Questions for Reflection and Discussion

1. Is increase, lift, progress, and growth a regular part of your spiritual life? Are there steps you can take to experience more growth?
2. It is understandable that Christians desire increase. However, this does not mean that we should look down on small things. Consider this passage: "Do not despise these small beginnings, for the Lord rejoices to see the work begin" (Zech. 4:10, *NLT*). How does this verse apply to us today, and what should our attitude be when God has given us seemingly small assignments or provision? What did Jesus teach about how we treat small things? (Hint: See the parable of the talents beginning in Matthew 25:14).

3. According to Deuteronomy 8:5-18, what is one of the potential dangers that people face when they have experienced increase?
4. Speaking of Jesus, John the Baptist said, "He must increase, but I must decrease" (John 3:30). In what ways and at what times is it appropriate for us to decrease?
5. Why should the Christian not be afraid of increase? What are the positive aspects of increasing? What are some of the reasons God desires to increase his children?
6. Think back through the teaching in this chapter about the God of increase. List one thing you learned and one thing you can do right now that will allow you to begin accessing more of God's resurrection power—his *lift*—in your life.

CHAPTER SIXTEEN

Learning To Be a Lifter

"If you want to lift yourself up, lift up someone else."
– Booker T. Washington

God lifts us. That has been the theme of this book. But God also wants *us* to be lifters—maybe that's because we were created in his image and likeness (Gen. 1:26). God lifts us, and he tells us things to lift:

- Lift up your eyes to the Lord (Ps. 123:1).
- Lift up your souls (Ps. 25:1; 86:4; 143:8).
- Lift up your hands (Ps. 63:4; 1 Tim. 2:8).
- Lift up your faces to God (Job 22:26).
- Lift up your voices (Isa. 24:14).
- Lift up your heads (Luke 21:28).
- Lift up your eyes and look at the harvest (John 4:35).

All of these are important, of course, and many have to do with our devotion and consecration to God.

There is another "lift up" admonition in Scripture that is also very important, but it has to do with our relationships with one another. Solomon speaks of the danger of isolation and the benefits of partnerships, stating, "If they fall, the one will lift up his fellow. But woe to him who is alone when he falls and has not another to lift him up!" (Ecc. 4:10, *AMP*). We see a very practical application of this in Paul's remarks to a group of believers:

GALATIANS 6:1-3 (*NLT*)

1 Dear brothers and sisters, if another believer is overcome by some sin, you who are godly should gently and humbly help that person back onto the right path. And be careful not to fall into the same temptation yourself.

2 Share each other's burdens, and in this way obey the law of Christ.

3 If you think you are too important to help someone, you are only fooling yourself. You are not that important.

It is important to lift our hands and voice in worship, and to lift our soul up to God, but it is also important that we operate in humility and lift up each other.

God's lifting nature—his resurrection life—is not something that he wants to simply *extend to us*; it is also something that God wants to *express through us*. We should not dismiss as mere cliché the saying, "God blesses us to make us a blessing." Neither should we take lightly the phrase, "If God can get it *through* us, God will get it *to* us." God's plan and desired pattern for our lives is revealed in Jesus' words, "Freely you have received, freely give" (Matt. 10:8). Everything about God is designed to lift us—his love, his compassion, his mercy. Even his corrections are designed not to put us down but so "that we may be partakers of His holiness" (Heb.

12:10) and ultimately walk higher with him. Since everything about God is designed to ultimately lift us up, then all that God does through us should result in our lifting others as well.

This principle of "being lifted in order to lift" is clearly seen in Paul's statement to the Corinthians:

> **2 CORINTHIANS 1:3-4**
> **3 Blessed be the God and Father of our Lord Jesus Christ, the Father of mercies and God of all comfort,**
>
> **4 who comforts us in all our tribulation, that we may be able to comfort those who are in any trouble, with the comfort with which we ourselves are comforted by God.**

God places us in relationships with the intent that they will be mutually beneficial. We need what other people have to give, and other people need what we have to give. Paul articulates God's wise plan as he writes, "When we get together, I want to encourage you in your faith, but I also want to be encouraged by yours" (Rom. 1:12, *NLT*). God designed the Body of Christ to be a place where all the members assume the responsibility of lifting and encouraging one another!

One of the most powerful principles in the New Testament is found in the frequent usage of the phrase "one another" to describe how believers are beholden to care for and minister to one another. Consider the following scriptural directives:

- Love one another (John 13:34).
- Be devoted to one another (Rom. 12:10, *NIV*).
- Honor one another (Rom. 12:10, *NIV*).
- Live in harmony with one another (Rom. 12:16, *ESV*).
- Build up one another (Rom. 14:19, *NET*).

- Welcome and receive one another (Rom. 15:7, *AMP*).
- Admonish one another (Rom. 15:14).
- Be considerate of one another (1 Cor. 1:10, *MSG*).
- Be reverent and courteous with one another (1 Cor. 11:33, *MSG*).
- Care for one another (1 Cor. 12:25).
- Serve one another (Gal. 5:13).
- Bear one another's burdens (Gal. 6:2).
- Show tolerance for one another (Eph. 4:2, *NAS*).
- Be kind to one another (Eph. 4:32).
- Forgive one another (Eph. 4:32; Col. 3:13).
- Submit to one another (Eph. 5:21).
- Treat one another as more important than yourself (Phil. 2:3, *NET*).
- Be gentle and forbearing with one another (Col. 3:13, *AMP*).
- Teach and help one another (Col. 3:16, *JB Phillips*).
- Increase and overflow in love for one another (1 Thess. 3:12, *HCSB*).
- Comfort one another (1 Thess. 4:18).
- Edify one another (1 Thess. 5:11).
- Do good to one another (1 Thess. 5:15, *ESV*).
- Encourage one another (Heb. 3:13, *NAS*).
- Be concerned about one another (Heb. 10:24, *HCSB*).
- Motivate one another (Heb. 10:25, *NLT*).
- Look after one another (Heb. 12:15, *AMP*).
- Confess your trespasses to one another (James 5:16).
- Pray for one another (James 5:16).
- Have compassion for one another (1 Pet. 3:8).
- Be hospitable to one another (1 Pet. 4:9).

This is an amazing list, isn't it?

Think how attractive the Church would be to the world if believers deliberately practiced these principles at a high level. Imagine the tremendous amount of "lift" that would exist in our churches if Christians habitually cared for and encouraged one another the way these verses direct.

These are not legalistic obligations for the believer, but rather, these are the behaviors that will flow out of us when we recognize that "the love of God has been poured out in our hearts by the Holy Spirit who was given to us" (Rom. 5:5). When we yield to the influence and outworking of God's love, these "one another admonitions" are descriptions of how we will act toward one another.

When I think of people who are great encouragers, three biblical examples instantly come to mind. I believe these men powerfully and effectively embodied this "one another" principle. Let's take a closer look at these three individuals.

Barnabas: Son of Encouragement

Students of the Bible will quickly recognize Barnabas as Paul's friend and partner in ministry. Some do not realize that his real name was Joses. "Barnabas," which means *Son of Encouragement*, was a nickname given to him by the apostles because of his character (Acts 4:36). The nickname was so fitting—and Barnabas was so good at lifting—that the world now knows him by that name! Through his consistent attitude and actions, Barnabas regularly helped others experience greater elevation in life. The first time we see Barnabas encouraging others involves his generosity toward the work of God. Barnabas sold land that he owned and "brought the money and laid it at the apostles' feet" (Acts 4:37). While the money itself was a necessary tool enabling the Church to accomplish its work, the heart behind the gift—the generous and loving nature of Barnabas—must have been a tremendous encouragement to the apostles and the whole Body of believers.

A second example of the encouraging nature of Barnabas is seen when Saul of Tarsus got saved. Saul (later known as Paul) had ravaged the Church with fierce persecution, and believers understandably wanted to avoid him in every way possible. Acts 9:26 reads, "When Saul arrived in Jerusalem, he tried to meet with the believers, but they were all afraid of him. They did not believe he had truly become a believer" (*NLT*). The very next verse communicates the uplifting and hopeful nature of Barnabas.

ACTS 9:27 (*MSG*)
27 Then Barnabas took him under his wing. He introduced him to the apostles and stood up for him, told them how Saul had seen and spoken to the Master on the Damascus Road and how in Damascus itself he had laid his life on the line with his bold preaching in Jesus' name.

Barnabas was not only a lifter and encourager, but he was also a bridge-builder and a fence-mender. He believed in people and saw the best in them.

Shortly after Barnabas' encounter with Saul, we see him in action again. The Gentiles had begun to receive the gospel, and many of the Jewish believers in Jerusalem were skeptical about the validity of the Gentiles' experience. Some believed that in order for the Gentiles to get saved, they would first have to become circumcised and comply with the entire Law of Moses.

Can you imagine being a Gentile who had just received the good news of Jesus Christ? You've been told that eternal life is available to you as a free gift through Jesus' death, burial, and resurrection. When you put your trust in Jesus, you receive forgiveness and come into covenant with God. But then some very religious people say, "Not so quick. There are many rules and regulations you need to comply with before you can have a relationship with God." Such a view was not only false, but it would have also been tremendously disheartening to the new converts. If accepted, this legalistic view would certainly have distorted the very essence of the gospel message they had first received.

The leaders in the Jerusalem did a very wise thing when they heard that Gentiles were receiving the gospel, and it involved Barnabas.

ACTS 11:22-24 (*NLT*)
22 When the church at Jerusalem heard what had happened, they sent Barnabas to Antioch.

23 When he arrived and saw this evidence of God's blessing, he was filled with joy, and he encouraged the believers to stay true to the Lord.

24 Barnabas was a good man, full of the Holy Spirit and strong in faith. And many people were brought to the Lord.

Barnabas was able to see the good in the people. He didn't focus on the cultural differences between Gentiles and Jews. He didn't get upset over non-essential issues such as diet or observance of holy days. Rather, he saw God's grace at work, and he affirmed the Gentiles and celebrated with them over what God had done in their lives. Barnabas' lifting and encouraging nature resulted in much good fruit. Church history could have been very different had the Jerusalem Church sent someone to Antioch who did not possess the gracious heart and keen insight of Barnabas.

The fourth time we see Barnabas living up to his nickname (Son of Encouragement) involves his cousin Mark. Young Mark (sometimes called

John Mark) had gone with Paul and Barnabas on their very first missionary journey, but halfway through, Mark dropped off the team (Acts 13:13). Sometime later, when Paul and Barnabas were going to take another missionary journey, Barnabas desired to give Mark a second chance, another opportunity to serve. However, Paul was adamant that Mark had disqualified himself from being on their team and refused to allow Mark to join them. Acts 15:39 states, "Their disagreement was so sharp that they separated. Barnabas took John Mark with him and sailed for Cyprus" (*NLT*).

Scholars disagree about who was right in this specific quarrel between Paul and Barnabas, and it is not my purpose to go into that discussion here. What I do want to stress is that while Paul certainly had great success after this, becoming a giant in the Early Church, God ultimately brought much good out of the care and encouragement that Barnabas provided for Mark.

We can only imagine what happened when Barnabas took Mark to Cyprus. I have no doubt that Barnabas comforted, restored, encouraged, and mentored Mark until he became a vital part of Church history himself. Peter later refers to Mark as a spiritual son (1 Pet. 5:13) and history tells us that the gospel that bears Mark's name is really a compilation of the stories that Peter told him as they traveled and labored together in the gospel. Furthermore, Paul himself later requests that Mark come to him and notes that "he will be helpful to me in my ministry" (2 Tim. 4:11, *NLT*).

What a difference an encourager makes! Barnabas may not be as visible or famous as some of the other heroes in the Bible, but he played a vital role by lifting others. Every time we see him in Scripture, he is demonstrating a generous, caring, optimistic, and encouraging spirit. He made everyone else around him better. We need a host of people like Barnabas in the Church today!

The Ministry of Onesiphorus

Another great lifter even less known than Barnabas is an individual named Onesiphorus. Only mentioned twice in the New Testament, Onesiphorus nevertheless played a very important and deeply appreciated role in Paul's life. While we know that Paul constantly ministered to others, we see a few times in Scripture when Paul was the recipient of encouragement from others. One of these instances is recorded in the very last letter Paul wrote—Second Timothy. In this epistle, Paul is facing imminent death in a Roman prison and has been abandoned by many of his friends. Onesiphorus, though, was a very bright spot in an otherwise very dark set of circumstances. Paul writes:

2 TIMOTHY 1:15-18 (*NLT*)

15 As you know, everyone from the province of Asia has deserted me—even Phygelus and Hermogenes.

16 May the Lord show special kindness to Onesiphorus and all his family because he often visited and encouraged me. He was never ashamed of me because I was in chains.

17 When he came to Rome, he searched everywhere until he found me.

18 May the Lord show him special kindness on the day of Christ's return. and you know very well how helpful he was in Ephesus.

When everyone else was bailing on Paul, Onesiphorus searched diligently and found him. He actually traveled from another continent just to bring Paul some comfort, companionship, and fellowship—all of this meant the world to Paul! Onesiphorus also encouraged and lifted Paul when Paul faced great challenges in Ephesus.

One of the admirable traits of Onesiphorus is that he was not ashamed of Paul's chains. In Paul's case, these were literal chains due to his physical imprisonment. But many people have chains in the figurative sense. They struggle under chains of oppression, bondage, addictions, and so forth. Such people often desperately need the encouragement of others. They need caring people to support them, people who will not condemn them or turn away from them because of their "chains." Someone once said that if you want to find out who your real friends are, just have a crisis. Onesiphorus walked into Paul's life when everyone else was walking out. That is what made him a true friend and a true encourager.

I heard a delightful story years ago about a Sunday School teacher who was teaching the class about friendship. She decided to use Onesiphorus as an example of a true friend, and she asked one of the young students to read Second Timothy 1:15-18. When the student came to the name "Onesiphorus," he was uncertain how to pronounce it, so he tried to enunciate it phonetically. He ended up pronouncing the name as "One – is – for – us." That's not the right pronunciation, but it sure makes a great point! When we are struggling in life, we can be greatly lifted and encouraged just knowing that "One is for us."

The Presence of Titus

On another occasion, Paul benefitted from the encouragement of Titus. Paul had already endured many hardships in his ministry and had more threats to be concerned about, but he was also deeply concerned about his relationship with the Corinthian Church. To say that the relationship was strained is an understatement, and Paul was very troubled about it. (When you care about others, you do not want there to be uneasiness, friction, or strife in the relationship.) Fortunately, Paul received good news, and that good news came from Titus.

Notice that Paul remarks about God's uplifting and encouraging nature when he writes, "Then the God who lifts up the downcast lifted our heads and our hearts with the arrival of Titus" (2 Cor. 7:6, *MSG*). Titus was no doubt an encourager, but it was really the news of reconciliation that Titus brought from the Corinthians that was so helpful to Paul.

2 CORINTHIANS 7:7 (*NLT*)

7 His presence was a joy, but so was the news he brought of the encouragement he received from you. When he told us how much you long to see me, and how sorry you are for what happened, and how loyal you are to me, I was filled with joy!

Good news lifts the recipient of that news. Proverbs 25:25 expresses this concept well, saying, "As cold water to a weary soul, so is good news from a far country." It is a privilege to be a peacemaker and a part of reconciling others, even if it's just in terms of relaying a positive message.

If Titus had received different information from the Corinthians—if they were not repentant and positive toward Paul, Titus' job would have been more difficult. Paul would not have found the *information* encouraging, but I think Titus himself would have still endeavored to lift Paul's spirits. I believe Titus would have encouraged Paul to continue to trust God for a more positive outcome in the future and reminded him about the many believers whom Paul had positively influenced—who *did* receive his ministry with great appreciation. It is possible to have an encouraging *spirit* even when we don't necessarily have encouraging *information.*

God wants to lift each of us individually, but he also desires for "lift" to be pervasive throughout our relationships in the Body of Christ. God designed us to be a *lifted* people but also a *lifting* people. We clearly see this in the multitude of "one another" scriptures, as well as in the sterling examples of biblical characters such as Barnabas, Onesiphorus, and Titus.

❗ A Resurrection Declaration

God, you have lifted me. You raised me up with Christ and commissioned me to walk in the newness of his resurrection life. You have also called me to be a lifter. To you, I lift up my soul, my eyes, my hands, my head, my face, and my voice. I also lift up my eyes, as you instructed, to see the harvest—those in the earth needing the good news. You have also admonished me in your Word to lift up others, and to comfort others as you have comforted me. You have given me responsibilities in this life, not just to worship you, but to love, encourage, edify, and serve others around me. Help me to lift others. Help me be like Barnabas—a son of encouragement, and to be like others who offered encouragement and support to Paul. Thank you for helping me to be an effective lifter. In Jesus' name, I pray—amen.

Bonus Quotes

"There is a loftier ambition than merely to stand high in the world. It is to stoop down and lift mankind a little higher."

—Henry Van Dyke

"People will forget what you said, people will forget what you did, but people will never forget how you made them feel."

—Maya Angelou

"If I had my life to live over, I would spend more time encouraging others."

—F. B. Meyer

"One of the highest of human duties is the duty of encouragement…It is easy to discourage others. The world is full of discouragers. We have a Christian duty to encourage one another."

—William Barclay

"Sometimes our light goes out but is blown into a flame by another human being. Each of us owes deepest thanks to those who have rekindled this light."

—Albert Schweitzer

 Lyrics that Lift: Hymns of the Resurrection

From "At the Feet of Jesus" by Philip P. Bliss (1876)

At the feet of Jesus,
In that morning hour,
Loving hearts, receiving
Resurrection power,

Haste with joy to preach the word;
"Christ is risen, praise the Lord!"
At the feet of Jesus, risen now for me,
I shall sing His praises through eternity.

 Questions for Reflection and Discussion

1. Review Second Corinthians 1:5 and describe what God intends for our lives after he has helped us, comforted us, and strengthened us through life's challenges. Are we simply called to be recipients of God's help, or does he desire something from us as well?
2. Review the extensive "one another" list on pages 233-234. Are some of these "assignments" easier for you than others? When it comes to ministering to people, which two or three of these directives come most naturally to you? Which two or three do you find more challenging to do?
3. Explain why Joses received the nickname "Barnabas" (the Son of Encouragement). Do you think Barnabas possessed a special "gift of encouragement," or could every believer become better at encouraging and lifting others if they applied themselves to the task?
4. Do you think churches as a whole would become more appealing to people in the world if there was more encouragement and lifting taking place among believers? What would need to happen in order for believers to excel more in the area of encouraging others?
5. Is there someone who has been a Barnabas to you? Has someone been an Onesiphorus, walking into your life with encouragement when others were walking out? How did that person help you? Is there someone for whom *you* need to be a Barnabas? Do you need to be an Onesiphorus to someone you know?
6. Think back through the teaching in this chapter about learning to be a lifter. List one thing you learned and one thing you can do right now that will allow you to begin accessing more of God's resurrection power—his *lift*—in your life.

Conclusion

In the first few pages of Scripture, after God's glorious work of creation, man falls through disobedience. Paradise is lost to the first couple and their posterity. Through sin, a host of other ills (such as guilt, shame, fear, blame shifting, and alienation) insidiously entered the world and affected the human race. We must go back to the phrase that we discussed in chapter eight—*but God.*

Mankind chose sin and death, *but God* was determined to bring hope, life, and (eventually) resurrection to the ones he created. The rest of the Bible is a story of redemption—of God seeking to restore men and women to their once lofty place. The story unfolds over multiple generations and centuries, until Christ comes to raise us with himself. The story is relatively simple: Man dies; God brings life. Man falls; God lifts him up.

- The Old Testament shows the fall of man and presents the promise of new life, of resurrection to come.
- The gospels introduce Jesus as the God-Man who breaks into our space-time world from eternity to actually *be* the Resurrection and the Life to all who trust him.
- The Book of Acts displays men coming back to life through the power of the glorious gospel and the working of the Holy Spirit.
- The Epistles explain how men come to life through Christ and how they can walk progressively and increasingly in a new, elevated life.
- The Book of Revelation presents the consummation of all things, including the death of death, and the ultimate supremacy of life and lift in the Paradise of God (Rev. 2:7).

The Bible essentially teaches that our spiritual nature can experience resurrection *right now*. If we have accepted Jesus as our Lord, we have already been spiritually raised with Christ to walk in newness of life (Rom. 6:4).

While we are in these physical bodies, mortal though they are, we can experience progressive degrees of lift (or resurrection life) as we walk in the Spirit and according to God's Word. The gradual nature of our spiritual growth in lift is found in such biblical phrases as "going from strength to strength," "from faith to faith," and "from glory to glory" (Ps. 84:7; Rom. 1:17; 2 Cor. 3:18). This spiritual growth takes place as we eagerly anticipate the day of ultimate lift—the transformation and glorification of our physical bodies.

The first three chapters of the Book of Revelation deal with first-century churches in Asia Minor (modern Turkey). Jesus encourages them, challenges them, warns them, and admonishes them. The practical instruction in these chapters is still of great benefit to churches today. The fourth chapter continues to offer a message of great benefit to us, opening with a decided change in tone and focus:

> **REVELATION 4:1 (*NLT*)**
> **1 Then as I looked, I saw a door standing open in heaven, and the same voice I had heard before spoke to me like a trumpet blast. The voice said, "Come up here, and I will show you what must happen after this."**

While this verse was a personal message to the Apostle John, the invitation "come up here" is something I believe we will all eventually hear, and if we listen to the Spirit of God, perhaps we will hear it even now.

No, God is not necessarily telling us to come to heaven at this very moment. We have work yet to do.

But I think God is saying to believers today, "Come up here—to a higher level of living. Come up here—think my thoughts after me. Come up here—to a place of spiritual maturity, to a place of walking more fully in the light of my Word. Come up here—allow me to help you walk more obediently, more faithfully, and more generously. Come up here—empowered by the outflow of Jesus' resurrection and filled with hope based on the resurrection yet to come."

God is here to lift us while we are still on this earth. The Lord invites us to look to him for lift every day of our life. The familiar song reminds us what will happen if we turn our eyes upon Jesus: "The things of earth will grow strangely dim in the light of his glory and grace."

PRAYER OF SALVATION

God loves you— no matter who you are, no matter what your past. God loves you so much that he gave his one and only begotten Son for you. The Bible tells us that "...whoever believes in him shall not perish but have eternal life" (John 3:16 NIV). Jesus laid down His life and rose again so that we could spend eternity with Him and experience His absolute best on earth. If you would like to receive Jesus into your life, say the following prayer out loud and mean it in your heart.

Heavenly Father, I come to you admitting that I am a sinner. Right now, I choose to turn away from sin, and I ask you to cleanse me of all unrighteousness. I believe that Your son, Jesus, died on the cross to take away my sins. I also believe that he rose again from the dead so that I might be forgiven of my sins and made righteous through faith in him. I call upon the name of Jesus Christ to be the Savior and Lord of my life. Jesus, I choose to follow You and ask You that You fill me with the power of the Holy Spirit. I declare that right now I am a child of God. I am free from sin and full of the righteousness of God. I am saved in Jesus' name. Amen.

If you prayed this prayer to receive Jesus Christ as your Savior for the first time, please contact us to receive a free book by writing to us.

www.harrisonhouse.com
Harrison House
PO Box 35035
Tulsa, Oklahoma 74153

The Harrison House Vision

Proclaiming the truth and the power

Of the Gospel of Jesus Christ

With excellence;

Challenging Christians to

Live victoriously,

Grow spiritually,

Know God intimately.